D0394787

Beyond
Blue

Therese J. Borchard

Author of the award-winning blog
"Beyond Blue" on Beliefnet. com

Beyond
Blue

Surviving Depression & Anxiety and Making the Most of Bad Genes

CENTER
STREET.

NEW YORK BOSTON NASHVILLE

To the best of my ability, I have re-created events, locales, people, and organizations from my memories of them. In order to maintain the anonymity of others, in some instances I have changed the names of individuals and places, and the details of events.

Grateful acknowledgment is made to the following for permission to reprint previously published material:

Vintage Books, a division of Random House, Inc. for excerpts from *An Unquiet Mind* by Kay Redfield Jamison. Copyright © 1995 by Kay Redfield Jamison. Reprinted with permission of Vintage Books, a division of Random House, Inc.

Center Street
Hachette Book Group
237 Park Avenue
New York, NY 10017

Visit our website at www.centerstreet.com.

Center Street is a division of Hachette Book Group, Inc.
The Center Street name and logo are trademarks of Hachette Book Group, Inc.

Printed in the United States of America

First Edition: January 2010
10 9 8 7 6 5 4 3 2 1

Library of Congress Cataloging-in-Publication Data

Borchard, Therese Johnson.
    Beyond blue: surviving depression & anxiety and making the most of bad genes / Therese J. Borchard. — 1st ed.
       p. cm.
    ISBN 978-1-59995-156-0
    1. Borchard, Therese Johnson—Mental health. 2. Affective disorders—Patients—Biography. I. Title.
    RC537.B65 2009
    616.85'270092—dc22
    [B]
                                                            2009001159

For Eric, who kept me alive and never stopped loving me;

For Ann Omohundro, my guardian angel and first bipolar friend;

For Mike Leach, my mentor, who believed in me when I couldn't;

For my mom, who called me twice daily for a year;

For Michelle, who wrote 90 percent of the notes in my self-esteem file;

For Beatriz Castillo de Vincent, a soul sister;

*For Holly Rossi and Deb Caldwell,
the brilliant brains and partners behind Beyond Blue;*

*For my dear Beyond Blue readers,
especially those who have lost loved ones to suicide;*

*And for Dr. Milena Hruby Smith, my psychiatrist,
and the other doctors at the Johns Hopkins Mood Disorders Center,
who gave me my miracle.
Thank you.*

One should learn from turmoil and pain,
share one's joy with those less joyful
and encourage passion when it seems likely
to promote the common good.

—Kay Redfield Jamison

Contents

Part I

Drink, Pray, Cry
My Story

Part II

Beyond Blue

Or At Least Headed That Way

Prelude

The Black Hole of Bile

It's Not Forever

In 400 BC Hippocrates defined depression, or "melancholy" as it was called back then, with these words: *an excess of black bile.*

I concur, with just one more addition to his description: that depression is a yawning pit with no exit, rope, or ladder in sight, which is why it's so terrifying on top of being repulsive, repugnant, repellant, and all the other adjectives in my thesaurus that begin with R. I woke up in that bleak, nasty trench of sewage in the middle of the night, and every dawn, month after month.

I remember the morning I dragged it with me down the stairs and stared for a long time at a bowl of oatmeal and a cup of Starbucks on the kitchen table. I just stood there, with all the life of a statue in a strange and dangerous park. *For God's sake, would someone please tell me when this will end?!?*

It was supposed to be a happy day, when our son David would earn his last yellow stripe and get his yellow belt. Instead it went like this . . .

Five four-year-old boys were sitting in level-eight karate pose on the olive green and red padded mat of Evolutions Gym in Annapolis.

"Who knows the rules?" asked Mr. Joe, a black belt in Tae Kwon Do and a master tactical instructor.

"No pushing," yelled one karate midget.

"No talking," said another.

"We control what?" asked Mr. Joe.

"Our bodies," replied the kid with an orange belt.

"Our mouths," said everyone, cued by Mr. Joe holding his index finger over his mouth.

"And . . ." Mr. Joe pointed to his head.

"Our minds!" the five screamed.

If it were only that easy, I thought. I was fighting the usual war inside my head. Even though I had relegated twenty minutes in the evening to list in my journal all the negative messages I told myself, an exercise my therapist recommended, insults still sneaked into my head about once every half-second.

The boys hadn't even stood up before I began my battle against the voices.

You're stupid. You're lazy. You're weak.

I reached inside my jean pocket, clutched my medal of St. Therese, and fought back.

Shut up! Shut up! Please, God, be with me, I said, as I concentrated on my breathing.

Inhale, one, two, three, four. Exhale, one, two, three, four.

My daughter, Katherine, wouldn't leave the water cooler alone. A typical two-year-old, she was filling up paper Dixie cups with water and dumping them in the trash.

"Stop it!" I scolded her, picking her up. She threw a tantrum, of course, head and legs thrust backward. Two moms shot me the "you have no control over your kid—you're an upcoming episode of *Supernanny*" look.

Stressed out, I headed to the playroom, or the "pinkeye pit," designed for difficult siblings of disciplined karate kids.

You're a horrible mother. You suck at it. You're not cut out for it. You're not cut out for anything. Except for maybe killing yourself. But you'd probably fail at that, too, if you ever got up the courage.

I fought back again. *Stop it! I'm a good mom. Concentrate on your thoughts. Appreciation. Appreciation. Think of everything you have to be grateful for.*

According to Dan Baker, coauthor of *What Happy People Know*, appreciation is the antidote to fear, and fear—of not having enough or not being enough—causes depression and anxiety.

I tried to do what Baker calls the Appreciate Audit. I thought about all the things I was thankful for.

I didn't know where to start.

I had money to pay for this stupid karate class. I had two healthy kids, one so healthy he could kick the hell out of the sheet of plastic Mr. Joe held up for him, and the other so healthy I could barely restrain her during a tantrum. I had all my limbs: legs to walk over to the water cooler to pull Katherine out of the trash can, and arms to tie David's white belt with nine yellow stripes. I had all my senses, vision to see Katherine filling her sixth Dixie cup with water, vision to see the stares from the other moms who apparently had never experienced a tantrum in public.

I was only three items into my gratitude list when I caught sight of a mom plugging away at her laptop computer. Her son was seated at the kids' table reading his copy of *I'm So Well Behaved Because My Mommy's Not a Whackjob.*

Now there's a mom who can multitask. You could never do that. You'll never write again. You couldn't hold a job if you wanted to. You'll never amount to anything. Why don't you just end it right now . . . so you can at least give your kids the chance to grow up without you—without the poison that your existence is to them.

I started to fight back again but felt defeated. My eyes were wet, ready to burst into a rather ugly Niagara Falls at any minute.

Come on. Don't give in. Control your thoughts. Be grateful, damn it!

My stomach began to shake, then my legs. Before I knew it, I was trembling like my grandmother used to in her kitchen, chain-smoking as she cooked, and on the verge of a bona fide panic attack.

Look at you. You are pathetic. You can't control your thoughts. How are you going to drive home like this? See, this is what I mean. Get out of your kids' life right now! Don't stick around and ruin everything for them.

Visibly shaking and with tears now running down my face, I picked up Katherine and headed to the bathroom.

On the way I read all the inspirational framed prints that lined the wall outside the main gym.

The first one was about determination. On the bottom of an image of runners crossing the finish line was a quote by Eleanor Roosevelt: "Believe in yourself. . . . You must do that which you think you cannot do."

But what if you can't, Eleanor!?! I shouted silently to the framed quote, still holding Katherine as proof of one good thing I had done with my life. *What if no matter how hard you try to train your thoughts, they always turn to death, to suicide, as the only way out . . . as the only path to peace inside this horrible brain? What if all the energy and effort you put into being so goddam grateful makes you want to die even more? Because the more you try, the more you fail. AND THE MORE YOU FAIL, THE MORE YOU HATE YOURSELF!*

Once inside the ladies' room, I put Katherine down on the cobalt spongy floor and sat down on a bench to try to control my breathing. I had forgotten the paper bag that I usually carried in case of an attack. *Breathe in. One. Two. Three. Four. Visualize water. Breathe out. One. Two. Three. Four.*

"Mommy, are you sad?" Katherine asked me, as she hopped up on the bench to play with my ponytail.

I nodded, and then fetched some toilet paper to blow my nose.

"But I'll be okay, sweetie. Mommy has allergies that make her shake and cry and breathe funny," I explained. "But she's okay. Everything's fine."

We arrived back to the karate class in time to hear Mr. Joe tell the five kids to use their "black belt spirit." I felt like I had just flushed mine down the toilet, never to be retrieved. I couldn't hide my red eyes, but I was able to restrain further tears.

David bowed on his way to the front of the class to be awarded the yellow stripe. And then, upon directions from Mr. Joe, ran to give me a hug.

I was so desperate for someone to assure me that the torment would end, that the mother ship was on its way to earth with the human formerly known as Therese, and that Mama ET had apologized profusely for any inconvenience caused by her mistaking Therese with an alien-hybrid project.

I called my mom.

"It *will* pass. I promise," she said.

I phoned my friend Michelle.

"You *will* feel better," she assured me.

I talked to Mike, my writing mentor and foster dad.

"You won't always feel like this," he declared.

I cried to my guardian angel, Ann.

"Dump that pea-brained doctor and get to Johns Hopkins. *Then* you will get better," she instructed me.

And then I would read the paragraph of hope from William Styron's book *Darkness Visible* while listening to the soundtrack from *Rocky*:

> If depression had no termination, then suicide would, indeed, be the only remedy. But one need not sound the false or inspirational note to stress the truth that depression is

not the soul's annihilation; men and women who have recovered from the disease—and they are countless— bear witness to what is probably its only saving grace: it is conquerable.

That's why depressives need each other. We have to remind the suffering person that the Black Hole of Bile isn't a permanent place. Light is near. In fact, as Meister Eckhart wrote, "it is in the darkness that one finds the light, so when we are in sorrow, then this light is nearest of all to us."

There is hope. This book is about that light.

Confessions of a Holy Whackjob

Some people are born with jagged edges—restless and discontent with volatile moods and intense emotions—explained author and professor Kay Redfield Jamison in an essay broadcast on NPR's *This I Believe* series. And others emerged from their mothers' wombs with smooth lines and unbroken skin, grounded and peaceful. These Mr. Rogers types find contentment in the smallest and simplest of things (a bowl of instant oatmeal, a green cardigan sweater, a goldfish swimming to the surface to eat crumbs), while the Michael Jacksons among us—the creative but combustible artists—sit down to a gourmet feast at a five-star restaurant, only to bolt to the restroom three minutes later in a panic attack as their food gets cold.

That would be me.

Hi. I'm Therese. I'm a manic-depressive, an alcoholic, and an adult child of an alcoholic; a codependent, a boundaries violator, and a stage-four people pleaser; an information hoarder or a clutter magnet, an Internet abuser, and an obsessive-compulsive or ritual-performing weirdo; a sugar addict, a caffeine junkie, a reformed binge smoker, and an exercise fanatic; a hormonally imbalanced female, a PMS-prone time bomb, and a sexually dysfunctional or neutered creature; a workaholic, an HSP (highly sensitive person), and, of course, I'm Catholic. Which could possibly explain some of the above.

To most eyes I look normal, and I can behave normally, at least for two-hour intervals. No one would guess my insides to be so raw, or suspect that I was twice committed to a psych ward, was suicidal for close to two years, and considered electroconvulsive therapy (ECT) after the first twenty-two medication combinations failed. Then again, the more human beings I interview Barbara Walters–style, the more convinced I am that everyone struggles. There are just many layers, varieties, and degrees of strains inside the human psyche.

The difference between me and most of the civilized world is that they don't publish their insecurities, irrational fears, personality flaws, and embarrassing moments online and in print for everyone, including their in-laws and neighbors, to read.

Why on earth would I do that?

It has something to do with the twelfth step of most 12-step support groups I've attended, which is nearly all of them: to share my experience, strength (if you can call it that), and hope with others in order to secure some sanity for myself. Or, to use the language of the existentialist Søren Kierkegaard, the twelfth step is about getting cozy with our true selves, becoming "transparent under God" and vulnerable before others in order to form a bond of communion with those persons experiencing similar struggles.

There's nothing short of stripteasing that could get me more transparent under God and naked before readers, some of whom can be pretty mean—take the lady who called me a "bitter, complaining, self-serving, whiny white woman," not that I memorized her words—than writing my blog, Beyond Blue. Every day I write, *Full Monty* style, about my very imperfect recovery from everything, I expose all sorts of moles and cellulite patches to the public.

And you better bet there are ample freak-outs behind the scenes.

I obsess in the shower about what I should have left out. And I can't press Send without at least one good round of second-guessing about the Beyond Blue post in which I disclosed an ugly memory or an unbecoming quality of mine . . . jealousy, hypocrisy, and rage come to mind.

But then I'll get a note on the combox of a Beyond Blue post like this one from a reader named Wendi: "Thanks for being so open. I'm standing at the edge of the black hole, trying so hard not to fall in, and your courage and your vulnerability are inspiring me to keep going today." And I know it was the right thing to do, even if I'm walking with my tail, or computer, between my legs. Her sentiment makes risking public rejection and ridicule worth it, and encourages me to put myself out there yet another day.

Abraham Lincoln, one of my mental health heroes, knew something about the twelfth step. Two years before he became our country's sixteenth president, Mr. Emancipation wrote:

> The inclination to exchange thoughts with one another is probably an original impulse of our nature. If I be in pain I wish to let you know it, and to ask your sympathy and assistance; and my pleasurable emotions also, I wish to communicate to, and share with you.

In the early '90s, another fellow depressive, humorist Art Buchwald, candidly discussed his mood disorder and vacations at the psych ward on *Larry King Live* for this reason: "Celebrities [and insignificant people like me, he would add] can play a role in helping depressed people: When Bill Styron or Mike Wallace admit they struggled with depression, sufferers say, 'If they can have one, then I guess so can I.' Styron, for one, is a role model for me."

For an article in *Psychology Today* about celebrity meltdowns and famous people who have suffered from depression, Buchwald wrote this in his introduction: "Talking about depression seems to help me as much as the people I am talking to. I wouldn't want another depression in a million years but I have made peace with the two I have had."

But before getting undressed on the pages of Beyond Blue, I had to overcome a few reservations.

For one, I feared my symptoms were a strain of yuppie whining, because a white, American blonde who can afford to send her kids to Catholic school has no right to complain. Even if she's depressed.

Two million children in Africa die a year from Malaria.

That's suffering.

Mothers risk their lives to give birth in war-torn Iraq.

That's suffering.

Women in Darfur risk rape for their freedom.

That's suffering.

A stay-at-home mom with a three-bedroom house?

I don't think so.

But that's like saying the boy with an iPod shouldn't cry when he breaks his leg because his parents are loaded. Or my affluent neighbor who suddenly lost her husband to a heart attack last year is self-serving to grieve. Her money invalidates her pain, no?

I agree. I haven't walked a mile in an Afghan woman's sandals. And based on the headlines I read, I don't want to. I feel for her, and I pray for her. But it's unfair to say that I'm immune to pain because I'm white, American, and on a first-name basis with all the baristas at seven coffee houses in Annapolis.

If depression wasn't so painful, why would it be expected to be the second most debilitating disease worldwide by 2020, surpassed only by heart disease, and be considered by some experts more debilitating than many common medical conditions today, such as diabetes and arthritis? Why would thirty thousand Americans kill themselves each year? Why would suicide take more lives than traffic accidents, lung disease, or AIDS? Why would the World Health Organization rank suicide as the second-leading cause of death worldwide among females between the ages of fifteen and forty-four?

And I was afraid of appearing self-indulgent.

I've been in publishing long enough to know how personal blogs and memoirs are commonly perceived: "Enough about me. What do you think about me?" I've long wanted to write about my struggle with depression and anxiety, but I hesitated to become yet another self-absorbed writer. So I stuck to compilations, where I collected other authors' self-indulgent essays.

And then I realized that the articles and books that I most enjoyed—that helped me tremendously in my spiritual journey and recovery—were memoirs and personal essays. I didn't care that they were self-indulgent. In fact, I liked that they were self-absorbed. Because it freed me to be self-reflective, as well, and try to be a more loving person. Writers like Anne Lamott and Kathleen Norris and Erma Bombeck and Kay Redfield Jamison have instructed me with the lessons from their own lives.

I also hated labels. In calling myself a manic depressive, would I trap my psyche in sick mode? By accepting my diagnosis of bipolar disorder, would I prevent healing? By writing the words "I am mentally ill," or "I'm a holy whackjob," was I stifling the universe's energy flowing to and from my third chakra, eliminating all chances of reaching Nirvana? Was all this depression talk holding myself to a place that I was, but not where I am, or where I could go, annihilating any prospect of being reincarnated as the Dalai Lama?

"Like a diagnosis, a label is an attempt to assert control and manage uncertainty," writes Rachel Naomi Remen, M.D., one of the first pioneers in the mind-body health field. "It may allow us the security and comfort of a mental closure and encourage us not to think about things again. But life never comes to a closure, life is process, even mystery. Life is known only by those who have found a way to be comfortable with change and the unknown." The renowned medical intuitive Caroline Myss warns against a "woundology" that is rampant in our pharmaceutical-driven culture: the tendency to "define ourselves by our wounds" and to "burden and lose our physical and spiritual energy and open ourselves to the risk of illness."

I've come to disagree. My labels have freed me to live in better harmony with the person I wish to be. And besides, "wounded" people are so much more fun to hang out with than "flawless" folks who deny their illnesses and object to prescriptions. Because, for the large part, we wounded know how to laugh. And what freedom and humility and community there is in that laughter.

Finally, I was afraid of publicly disclosing my mood disorder because so few people understand depression today, even with that cool Zoloft commercial out—the one where the sad egg no longer wants to chase the butterfly, i.e., Humpty Dumpty before the fall. With depression, there's no visible cast or oxygen tank. Just a lame story about some bad thoughts.

In 2005—when I was stuck deep inside the Black Hole—I

bailed on delivering the keynote address to a large convention. My hands were trembling so badly with anxiety that I was having difficulty getting a spoonful of Cheerios to my mouth. Holding a microphone would have been problematic, not to mention uninspiring for the masses.

"I'm sorry," I explained in an e-mail to the events coordinator a few months before the conference. "I'm having some health problems."

I stayed vague because I was afraid that the woman wouldn't understand.

Like so many other people in my life.

Many months later the topic of depression made front-page news in Annapolis with the suicide of Phil Merrill, a renowned publisher, entrepreneur, and diplomat in the Washington area. Eleven days later Montgomery County Executive Douglas Duncan withdrew his candidacy for governor of Maryland because of his struggle with depression.

Articles cited all the people who had come out, past and present: Abraham Lincoln, Winston Churchill, Kay Redfield Jamison, Archbishop Raymond Roussin, Mike Wallace, William Styron, Art Buchwald, Robin Williams, Patty Duke, Kitty Dukakis, and Brooke Shields. Their reputations were still intact, so I began to think maybe writing about my inner demons wouldn't be the end of mine.

These folks went public to help others. Lincoln wanted people to know that his melancholy was a "misfortune, not a fault," and that his humor, his jokes, were the "vents of [his] moods and gloom." Churchill referred to his deep melancholy as his "black dog" (I prefer "mutt"). It was the teacher of perseverance. "Every day you may make progress," he wrote. "Every step may be fruitful. Yet there will stretch out before you an ever-lengthening, ever-ascending, ever-improving path. You know you will never get to the end of the journey. But this, so far from discouraging, only adds to the joy and glory of the climb."

The enlightened voices of Art and Abe became my guides as I felt my way, blindfolded, through the woods of depression and anxiety to the campfire, where a crowd of fellow depressives welcomed me. The words of Kay Redfield Jamison and Brooke Shields comforted me on those scary afternoons when I felt as though I'd never be freed from my sadness. Today they still reassure me that if I ever get sucked into that Black Hole again, it won't be forever. Moreover, without their perspective, I'd think I really was going crazy, that I was the fruitcake my twin sister called me in the fourth grade.

I owe it to these missionaries of truth to continue the chain of support: to write and speak on behalf of those impaired by bad brain chemistry—and disruption in the structure and function of neural circuits, as neurobiologists are learning—trying my best to strip mental illness of its unfair stigma.

But let me get something straight from the start: these pages aren't about my dispensing smart nuggets of wisdom from my vast reservoir of knowledge. If that were the case, the book would be found in the children's section at Borders, where all the 250-word manuscripts end up, and it would bore you to sleep—a rather good thing if you're in a manic cycle. Anyone pulling off that stunt is a dude you want to run from. With your children.

These pages provide the much-needed context to my blog, Beyond Blue. My editor and friend, Michelle, has graciously provided me the room to write the details of my story: like when I first noticed that my thoughts (*Kids are starving in Cambodia, and we have a trash crisis in the US!*) were different from my sisters' (*These jeans are cool, and I want to buy that CD!*), what I used to do about these thoughts (*collect everyone's milk money by making them feel guilty about the Cambodian kids; spend three hours in the confessional*), and why I did those things (*if I didn't, my chicken pox would never go away, leaving me with hideous scars as an adult*). You see, those anecdotes and more are difficult to tell in 750 words—the typical length of a Beyond Blue blog post. So I get thousands of words to describe them here!

The chapters are a neat and tidy regurgitation of the insidious monologues inside the noggin of a recovering "everything," spun in a light that I hope will encourage you. This book tells the story of an anxious and self-conscious woman who is trying like hell to do her best in this world with a brain that feels like Katherine's assembled-at-home Barbie tricycle, with its 3,297 parts and operating instructions in Chinese.

I have broken *Beyond Blue* into two parts. The first half, "Drink, Pray, Cry: My Story" reads like a memoir of a girl whose father must be a shrink, because she's been diagnosed with practically every illness covered in *The Diagnostic and Statistical Manual of Mental Disorders*, Fourth Edition (or *DSM-IV*). Here you'll read about the early seeds of my depression, how my mood disorder morphed into a different beast with every new US president, about my futile attempts at taming the beast, and about my miracle in the end.

In the second half, "Beyond Blue: Or At Least Headed That Way," I give you a tour inside my brain and introduce you to some of the demons that live there rent free. I share some techniques I've used to evict the cheap guys, and how I go about erecting all those damn boundaries in my life—with the cable guy, my FedEx delivery man, and with certain friends—so that I can continue down Recovery Lane.

The chapters will address my ongoing struggles to stay sane while also including topics that are ever on my radar: striving for a healthy marriage, caring for my kids when I feel incapable of caring for myself, maintaining good friendships and tossing out toxic ones, and of course my constant conversation with God, which most of the time goes like this: "Hey you, Big Guy, what the hell were you thinking with that one?"

There's something in here for everyone who has ever felt insecure, for all people except for, say, Tom Cruise. The reader need not have suffered through the mango breakdown that I did in order to relate to the discussions of codependency, people pleasing, and addiction that I produce in these pages.

My sincere intention for *Beyond Blue* is that anyone who struggles with anxiety or depression—even in the slightest way—might find a companion in me, some consolation in the incredibly personal details of my story, and a bit of hope to lighten an often dark and lonely place.

Although I have cussed out God too many times to count, asking him what kind of marijuana he was smoking the day he designed my brain, I agree with Kay Redfield Jamison, that "tumultuousness, if coupled to discipline and a cool mind, is not such a bad sort of thing. That unless one wants to live a stunningly boring life, one ought to be on good terms with one's darker side and one's darker energies."

I wish Helen Keller were wrong when she said, "We would never learn to be brave and patient if there were only joy in the world." Then again, what kind of world would we live in if everyone were content with instant oatmeal and green cardigan sweaters? If no one had to be excused to go to the ladies' room at the Tavern on the Green in order to breathe into a paper bag due to a fit of anxiety? If we were all born with smooth lines?

Snore. Thunderous, blaring, wear-the-nasal-strips-or-you-sleep-on-the-couch snore.

Before you dig into the details of my psyche, let me apologize in advance for any potentially offensive humor. I use sarcasm as a defense mechanism. Ten years of therapy taught me something. But I'm hanging on to it. No first step, fifth step, or twelfth step on that baby. I'm keeping the jokes and the acerbic tone because Abe and Art said wit was essential to sanity, that comedy can keep a person out of the psych ward (my inaccurate translation). And this is definitely true: if you're laughing, you're not crying, even though they look similar. And that works for me.

Part I

Drink, Pray, Cry

My Story

Chapter One

Prayer, Piety, and Panic

Depression in My Younger Years

T here is a Buddhist tale about a group of blind men trying to describe an elephant from different perspectives.

"Surely an elephant is like a pot," said the man touching the elephant's head.

"No," said the man holding an ear. "An elephant is like a winnowing basket."

The man feeling the tusk said it was a plowshare; the one clenching the trunk, a plow; the man at the foot, a pillar; the back, a mortar; the tail, a hose; the tuft of the tail, a brush.

That's what it's like describing my bipolar disorder.

I could tell you about my manic cycles, which my husband, Eric, says are like a litter of puppies running around in circles and chasing each other's tails. Or I could recount the details of my suicidal eighteen months, when I clutched my medal of St. Therese so hard it almost became embedded in my palm. I could start with my soul, my dark night, and how the light trickled in the way it does at dawn. Or I could describe the battlefield of my mind, where today team NIT (negative intrusive thoughts) is killing team PT (positive thoughts) 57 to 2.

I'm going to start with the elephant's girl parts, in particular its womb: with me, the fetus, sitting uncomfortably inside my mom's womb in my native town of Dayton, Ohio. Because the truth is that I don't ever remember *not* being anxious and depressed.

That's not to say I don't have happy childhood memories. There are plenty of those, and they are all documented in the cool photo albums my mom gave me and my sisters for Christmas three years ago: those autumn afternoons my twin sister and I would jump into a massive pile of leaves, undoing the hours of raking our neighbor did; summer trips to Baskin-Robbins and Friendly's, where my sisters and I would split a Reese's Pieces sundae with extra whipped cream; Easter Sundays, when the big rabbit would fill my basket with enough chocolate and jelly beans to last me to next year's basket; and magical Christmases. Given the estrogen levels at our house—produced by four sisters within three years of each other—we should have had Greek symbols over our garage, because it was like a sorority house on many occasions.

But I never remember a time when I was without angst.

My mom called me her "Velcro kid" because I stuck to her. As a preschooler, I remember being scared to death she was going to die every time she left the house: I loathed seeing her apply her very red lipstick because it signaled an imminent departure and the *clickety-clack* noise of the garage door raising sounded like taps. I would say good-bye forty times, and that was never enough.

Severe separation anxiety isn't abnormal for young kids. Especially those who are as ultrasensitive as I was. What delivered me into the weirdo category were the intrusive thoughts that made no sense: that I had to compliment the waitress on her curly perm or her yellow polyester uniform—or else something terrible would happen to me, like I would have to wear that yellow polyester uniform for the rest of my life, even to the prom. I obsessed about bizarre details, like where my tongue was positioned when I swallowed, as if I was somehow to blame for the Atlantic Ocean–sized gap between my two front teeth. Some preoccupations drove me to rituals like turning out the lights 2,876 times, washing my hands five times before dinner, looking under my bed for my shoes even though I had already checked eighty-seven times before, or skipping over and counting the cracks of a sidewalk on the way to school.

Even as a young child, I complained of "feelings" that stalked my every move—of being unworthy, afraid, and terribly ashamed—and obsessing about death as if it were a real option if I got that desperate. When I was thirteen, I wrote in my journal:

> I can't keep these feelings in any more. My mom doesn't understand. She tries but she doesn't. The world seems terrible to me. I think I need a psychologist badly. I have to keep busy to stay away from my feelings, and lately I haven't been busy. I have thought about suicide many times. It seems to always be on my mind.

Now sprinkle an ounce of Catholicism on top of that chemistry, and you have, *voila!* a religious nut!

Growing up Catholic, for me, was both a blessing and a curse.

A blessing in that my faith became a refuge for me, where my disordered thinking could latch onto practices and traditions that made me feel normal and secure. For this reason, I've always maintained that Catholicism is the most suitable religion for the mentally ill. Think about it. There is a saint for every neurosis: St. Joseph takes care of those prone to panic attacks while traveling. For twitching, Bartholomew the Apostle is the dude. Those roaming the house in their sleep can call on Dymphna. The venerable Matt Talbot is patron saint to those struggling with alcoholism and drug addiction. And, of course, St. Jude covers the hopeless causes.

Catholicism provided me with a safe place to go for comfort and consolation, to hear I wasn't alone, and that I would be taken care of. I kept my picture book of saints bookmarked to St. Therese of Lisieux, who, when she was dying "pressed her crucifix to her heart, and looking up to heaven said, 'I love Him! My God, I love You!'" and to Joan of Arc who was "taken to the marketplace of Rouen and burned to death. With her eyes on a crucifix, she cried out, 'Jesus, Jesus,' through the flames." *The saints have experienced much deeper agony than I have,* I reasoned as a young girl. *I should turn to them with my pain. Because if I can gaze at Jesus like they did, I will be protected from my thoughts.*

It made perfect sense that I would turn to the stories and ceremonials of my faith, because that was where my mom journeyed in her darkest hours, when I was eleven years old and my dad called a family meeting to announce he would be sleeping in a separate apartment for a while; that turned into three years and was followed by the devastating news that he was never coming home, and was, in fact, going to marry a woman seventeen years his junior. His younger bride, I suspect, tolerated his drinking scene more than my mom and didn't burden him with so much religion: weeping statues of the Virgin Mary on the bedroom dresser, the image of the Sacred Heart in the kitchen—which I still swear to this day smiled at me every time I cleared the table—the novenas to all the saints, and, oh, let's not forget the mammoth rosary hanging over the living room mantel, each bead the size of a grapefruit.

My mom named me after her favorite saint, St. Therese of Lisieux, or the Little Flower, because I am her favorite daughter. Not! Truthfully, she swears she hadn't felt so compelled to name her other babies in the way she was with me. Something about me even in utero, she vows, matched perfectly with the name Theresa.

The year of my parents' separation—when I was in fifth grade—I first witnessed the power of a novena to St. Therese. On the fifth day of five consecutive days of prayers—when tradition holds that the person praying will receive a shower of roses—our neighbor Mr. Miller, who kept an impeccable garden, was pruning his rose bushes. As he trimmed off the fully blossomed flowers to make room for the tender buds, he noticed my twin sister playing soccer in the backyard.

"Give these to your mom," he said, handing her at least eight dozen stunning roses: in vibrant shades of sapphire, indigo, daffodil, primrose, coral, and indigo, most of the petals perfectly formed and having just opened. With the determination and skills of an artist, my sister went back and forth, from his garden to our kitchen, arranging all the roses until she ran out of vases and counter space, making the place look like a Monet painting.

My mom dragged herself into the kitchen from the garage that evening, distraught and forlorn as she was so much of the time the year my dad left—the pangs of abandonment visible on her face—to find what looked and smelled like a heavenly rose garden. I'll never forget the tears of hope she cried when she remembered it was the fifth day of her novena.

But my religiosity was also a curse in that with all of its stuff—medals, rosaries, icons, statues—my faith disguised a serious mood disorder as piety. So instead of taking me to the school psychologist or to a mental health professional, the adults in my life considered me a very holy child, a religious prodigy, with a curiously intense faith.

Almost every anxiety and insecurity I felt as a kid fed into one fear: I wasn't pleasing God and was therefore going to hell.

I did everything in my repertoire of Catholic traditions and devotions to prevent that, of course. My bedtime prayers lasted longer than those recited by Benedictine monks; by the second grade, I had read the Bible start to finish, memorized key passages and made imaginary friends of all the primary characters: Jonah, Abraham, Moses, David, Joseph, Mary, and Elizabeth; I attended daily Mass, walking to church by myself each day; and every Good Friday I would camp out for five hours in my dad's den in the basement as I reenacted the Passion of Christ starring me as Judas, Jesus, Veronica, Simon, Mary, and every other major personality of the crucifixion scene.

During our closing liturgy at St. Charles Borromeo Elementary School in Kettering, Ohio, grades one to eight would sing "Let There Be Peace on Earth" for our principal, Sister Marie Karen. The last words of the song, "and let it begin with me," stuck to the gray matter of my brain and haunted me throughout the summer, so that I felt personally responsible for the cold war between the United States and Russia, and for the apartheid plaguing South Africa.

The slides of the starving people in Uganda—their protruding cheek bones and crooked teeth—shown as part of the Stations of the Cross during Lent, stayed with me well past Easter. On the weekends that my dad had us, he would give my sisters and me quarters to go play Pacman, that stupid arcade game, but I couldn't do it. Waste money that could feed a family in Somolia? The guilt was unbearable. So I saved my coins and gave them to Unicef. Besides, watching a big yellow dot gobble up smaller yellow dots fed my anxiety. Back then, I was a communist who found consumerism disturbing.

Two and a half decades later, I can see that to my junior high brain, having money—having the luxury of worrying about pimples and mean cliques in lieu of hunting for clean water and food in some African village—meant that I had no right to complain, and that I should always, without exception, wear a happy face. The fact that folks were hungry and dying of poverty in Zimbabwe translated into a no-tell policy that I was in great need of some counseling. *Because money should cure all. This was America!* Anything but a Colgate white smile was unacceptable. So I begged

God to be poor. Because then, and only then, I could disclose my pain.

For much of the same reason I desired to be a mystic. I looked at all the pain caused by my parents' divorce—in their lives and in my sisters' and mine—and I decided that I would never rely on anyone but God. That prescription for happiness was a perfect match to my interpretation of the Bible: that God needs to be Numero Uno, the Big Cheese, Mac Daddy—okay you get the point. So when we were roasting marshmallows during our first camping trip, and my Girl Scout buddies asked me who my boyfriend was, I replied, "God," which won me so much popularity and approval in those circles that I had no buddy with whom to go pee in the middle of the night. Apparently all the other Scouts had real boyfriends and didn't yet appreciate the benefits of befriending a Christian mystic.

"If you don't stop crying, I'm taking you to the hospital," my mom said to me when I was seven. She was scared herself, and she didn't know what to do with her daughter who would shriek with terror in the middle of the night, sitting up in her twin bed with beads of sweat dripping from her forehead as she held a pink plastic rosary in her hand.

You'd think the Hail Marys and Our Fathers I uttered while trying to fall asleep would protect me from the terror produced by my recurring dream. But it didn't. As soon as my head hit the pillow, the image was always the same: strings of rope or yarn swinging from left to right in a slow, methodical tempo like the needle of a metronome, gradually becoming entangled. They begin to creep toward me like the arms of an octopus. And then try to strangle me. I run away. And lose my breath. As all the rhythm evaporates into a rushed madness, I find myself perched atop balls of crinkled trash. I rest there for a moment, thinking I'm safe from the octopus arms. Until the balls come alive and try to crush me.

"It was only a dream," my mom would tell me, as I trembled and sobbed in her arms. "Dreams can't hurt you," she said, as she combed my thick hair with her fingers and wiped the tears from my eyes.

But I knew better. My dreams were prophecies . . . of fears that would come true, of order that would end in chaos, of messes that would destroy me, of my future.

I was afraid I would become my godmother, my aunt Mary Lou, who was my only exposure to mental illness.

In my mind, Mary Lou's responsibility to me as my godmother was far greater than catechism lessons, ensuring I received a proper religious education. She needed to do more than guide me spiritually and hold me at my Baptism. As a pious little girl whose biggest day of her life was her First Communion, I believed that one's godmother held the spirit of her goddaughter.

The way I saw it, my soul was eternally tied to my aunt Mary Lou's.

Which was terrifying.

Mary Lou started her life as a beauty. With dynamic features similar to Audrey Hepburn's, she was gorgeous. The second oldest after my mom of seven kids, she was the tallest, at five foot ten. And because of all her competitive ballet training, her height only added to her grace. In fact, she modeled through her adolescence, into high school.

All that changed when she went off to college. She fared okay at the small, all-women's college she attended in St. Louis. But during her junior year, the semester she spent in Rome, let's just say she did not do as the Romans do. She did as crazy people do in Rome: tossed her travelers' checks off the balcony to whomever was beneath; built an altar in her studio apartment there, believing that she was getting married; seeing and hearing things that were not there; and pretending she was different people, changing personalities every time the pope waved from his balcony.

Mary Lou's behavior was so neurotic in Rome that the police were called to transport her to the closest psych ward, where she was locked up. My grandfather then flew over to Rome with two doctors and two nurses, secured Mary Lou in a straitjacket and loaded her on the plane, and flew back with her to Dayton, where she immediately received shock therapy.

That hospital stay began the first of about twenty. And we're not talking the express version that yours truly had the benefit of. She was there for at least three months at a time, until a doctor could arrive at a diagnosis, most consistently bipolar disorder and schizophrenia, and a treatment plan. They'd eventually release her, sometimes after a year, once they felt she had stabilized. Sometimes she was able to hold a job for a full year. But usually it was only a few months before she ended up hospitalized again, strapped to the gurney, receiving electroconvulsive therapy all over again.

When she was manic, Mary Lou was the most generous godmother in the world. She would arrive at our doorstep bearing extravagant gifts. She bought me and my sisters 24-karat gold necklaces, gorgeous wool sweaters, and delicate porcelain dolls. I received twice as many gifts, of course, because I was Mary Lou's godchild. But I couldn't rip off the tags, because as soon as she dropped them off, my mom collected them from us and returned them to the stores, explaining that her sister was mentally ill and couldn't afford what she had purchased.

Then there were those other visits. At three in the morning, when Mary Lou stood outside our door shaking in the snow with no shoes, paranoid that people were coming after her. Even when she was locked up at the psych ward, my mom couldn't sleep soundly, because bars couldn't hold Mary Lou in. Once she was locked away in an institution twenty miles or so away. Completely psychotic, she escaped and hitchhiked her way back to Dayton and rang our front doorbell until my mom answered.

As the eldest of seven, it was usually my mom's job to take Mary Lou back to the hospital, to convince her that she needed to be treated again, even when the hospital treatments didn't seem to work. Most often, my mom and my grandpa would have to find yet another long-term program because Mary Lou's mom, my grandmother, was an active alcoholic at the time—and her drinking only escalated with Mary Lou's problems.

Each transition—from apartment to hospital—was perilous.

Because Mary Lou could turn on anyone trying to help her.

On one occasion, paranoid about people coming after her, she crashed in the front door of her apartment. Completely psychotic, she accosted my mom and dad, convinced they were plotting against her. Thankfully, with the help of some strangers, my parents forced her into the car. And she didn't jump out like she had done several times in my grandfather's car—which was why typically four people would need to take her to the hospital, one to guard each car door.

Once hospitalized, my mom would visit her several times a week. Sometimes she'd drag me and my sisters along with her. We'd sit there on the floor with our backs against a sterile white wall and wait for Mary Lou to say something.

She never did.

The time I was there alone I sat with three patients. They were like white ghosts, with no hint of emotions, feelings, or life. To this day, I can still see their faces, those vacant eyes, and feel the chills of that moment: when I saw for myself what mental illness can rob from a person who is treated incorrectly.

Where have their souls gone? I wondered. *How does a person get this way? Why does God do this to people?*

I internalized Mary Lou's cycles and her illness, in general, because I feared that therein lay my future: ordering off of a psych ward menu, with visiting hours from three to six. The wandering eyes, the blank expression . . . I'd get there one day, too.

"Am I like Aunt Mary Lou?" I asked my mom a million times growing up. "She was *different*. And I'm *different* like that, right?"

"No," my mom would immediately reply. "You and Mary Lou are nothing alike."

My mom had every right to deny the similarity: Mary Lou, her younger sister by two years, was schizophrenic, delusional, psychotic, and a host of other descriptions found in the *DSM-IV*. She spent more of her adulthood in a hospital room than in an apartment. From the time her illness fully exhibited itself at age twenty to the time she died at age forty-three, she was well for maybe seven years, if you lumped together all the good and stable times.

And her life ended in suicide, with a turn of the ignition key in my grandmother's garage.

I was sixteen years old at the time.

And I was devastated.

Because I saw so much of myself in my godmother.

It wasn't much of a leap for me to think I was crazy, too.

I'm not like Mary Lou in that I'm not schizophrenic and my bipolar disorder is not as severe as hers was. I also have the advantage of thirty years of medical and scientific research. But I am like my godmother in the very way I feared I would be as a young girl: in inheriting genes that predispose me to mental illness and to a brain chemistry that could have very easily ruined me by now, genes that hardwire a mind for mental anguish so that I have to chase after sanity each day—sometimes several times a day—with a dogged determination and a fierce tenacity I didn't know I had in me.

For Mary Lou's sake and for folks like her, who haven't been able to benefit from all the research and understanding of mental illness as I have, I dedicate my life to this cause: to making mental illness less scary for those who live it and to educating as many people as I can about mood disorders so that we can permanently remove the unfair stigma associated with depression and bipolar disorder.

I want to be Mary Lou's ambassador in this world, just as she is, and will always be, my godmother.

9 Ways to Stop Obsessing

The French call obsessive-compulsive disorder *folie de doute*, the doubting disease. That's what obsessions are—a doubt caught in an endless loop of thoughts. But even those not diagnosed with OCD can struggle with obsessions. In fact, I have yet to meet a depressive who doesn't ruminate, especially in our age of anxiety. Every day gives sensitive types like myself plenty of material to obsess about. So I'm constantly pulling out the tools that I've acquired over time to win against my thoughts, to develop confidence—the antidote to doubt—to take charge of my brain. Maybe they'll work for you, too.

1. *Name the beast.* My first step to tackle obsessions: I identify the thought. *What is my fear? What is my doubt?* I make myself describe it in one sentence, or, if I can, in a few words.
2. *Pencil it in.* Awhile back, when I was especially tormented by some obsessions, my therapist told me to schedule a time of day where I was free to ruminate. That way, she said, when you get an obsession, you can simply tell yourself, "Sorry, it's not time for that. You'll have to wait until eight in the evening, when I give you, My Head, fifteen minutes to obsess your heart out."

3. *Laugh at it.* Laughter can make almost any situation tolerable. And you have to admit, there is something a little funny about a broken record in your brain. I have a few people in my life who struggle with obsessions in the same way I do. Whenever I can't stand the noise in my head anymore, I call up one of them and say, "They're baaaaaack . . ." And we laugh.

4. *Throw it away.* One behavioral technique that works is to write out the obsession on a piece of paper. Then crinkle it up and throw it away. That way you have literally thrown out your obsession. Or try visualizing a stop sign. When your thoughts go there, remember to stop! Look at the sign!

5. *Learn the lesson.* I often obsess about my mistakes. I know I messed up, and I'm beating myself over and over again for not doing it right the first time, especially when I have involved other people and hurt them unintentionally. If that's the case, I will ask myself: *What is the lesson here? What have I learned?* Then I will describe the lesson that I have absorbed in one sentence or less.

6 *Reel it in.* Buried within an obsession are usually pieces of truth. But other parts are as accurate as a juicy celebrity tabloid story: "Celine Dion meets ET for drinks." That's why you need some good friends that will help you separate fact from fiction. When I call up my friend Mike and tell him my latest obsession, he usually laughs out loud and says something like this: "Wow. Reel it in, Therese. Reel it in. You are way out this time."

7. *Imagine the worst.* I know this seems wrong—like it would produce even more anxiety. But imagining the worst can actually relieve the fear triggering an obsession. Because you've hit bottom. You can't sink any lower! Isn't that refreshing?

8. *Put it on hold.* Sometimes I start to obsess about a situation for which I don't have enough information. So I put my obsession

on hold, like it's a pretty lavender dress at a boutique that I saw and want but don't have enough money to buy. So it's there, waiting for me, when I get enough dough—or enough data.

9. *Interrupt the conversation.* An obsession is like a conversation over coffee: "This is why he hates me, and this, too, is why he hates me, and did I mention why he hates me? I'm sure he hates me." So I can be myself and rudely interrupt. I don't even have to say, "Excuse me." I can ask a question or throw out another topic. And, best of all, no one will tell me, "Let her finish."

Chapter Two

BMI (Body Mass Issues)

Depression in My Thighs

As a young girl, religious scrupulosity provided me a twisted but effective way to assert some control over the chaos in my mind and, especially after my parents' split, the mess of my home life. I have no doubt that my predispositions to mental illness were so strong that anything as slight as picking up lice at school would have triggered symptoms. So I don't fault my mom and dad.

But one theory of depression suggests that any major disruption early in life, like trauma, abuse, or neglect, may contribute to permanent changes in the brain that lead to an overproduction of cotropin-releasing factor (CRF), which in turn stimulates the pituitary gland to release hormones that cause depression. According to the psychiatric geneticist James Potash, MD, stress can trigger a cascade of steroid hormones that likely alters the hippocampus—belonging to the brain's limbic system, the seat of human emotions—and retard its new growth. While most of my neurosis was probably tucked away in the "special" DNA God reserved just for me, I do think my parents' divorce and my mom's grief over the end of her marriage contributed to my cuckoo-bird manifestations.

Obsessive-compulsive disorder is about control more than anything. Once considered a rare mental disorder, it now afflicts up to

6.5 million people, making it one of the more common (or should we say *popular*, as if it's an ingredient on top of a pizza?) mental illnesses.

My mom must have known that miniature OCDish control freaks excel at activities like ballet and piano. She receives five stars for channeling my neurosis into worthwhile hobbies that I could focus on instead of God and how many rosaries I needed to pray to win his approval.

Music, particularly, became a powerful medium of self-expression for me. In practicing my cadences, scales, and arpeggios—and in learning how to play Bach's Concerto in D Minor and other classics—I found a safe, predicable place. Moreover, in creating rhythm and melody on a piano keyboard, I achieved an illusion of control.

But an adolescent girl prone to perfectionism who aspires to become a professional ballerina is guaranteed to develop an eating disorder by the time she's competing in spelling bees, around the eighth grade.

I was right on schedule.

By the time I reached junior high, I had managed to transfer all my obsessions about hell and sin to my diet and losing weight, pursuing the figure of a skeleton like the rest of the ballerinas at the studio.

So I danced for several hours after school in an intensive ballet program. Then I came home, tried to skip dinner, and worked out for another hour, usually jumping all over my family room—a kind of private aerobics—to the soundtrack of *Footloose*. At supervised meals I dropped my food into a napkin and threw it away. I wore layers of long underwear underneath my pants to so that my jeans didn't hang off my hips as a large neon sign to my mom: "Get this chick to a doctor!"

I would make up excuses to get out of Monday night dinners, our night with Dad after the divorce, and when I knew it was

unavoidable, I seated myself the farthest away from my father and
ordered items that I could easily dump into my lap.

I remember dropping an expensive salmon dinner into my cloth
napkin at the dinner table of a gourmet steak joint right before the
freshman father-daughter dance. After I carried my bundle to the
ladies' room, I panicked because the one trash can was empty with
no lid. The salmon would stand out. Hell, it might even jump out.
So I spent a considerable amount of time in there, wrapping the
fish and capers, finished with a delicious lemon-olive sauce, in toilet paper before disposing it, in case my sisters used the restroom
after me and found the poor salmon in the can.

On my sixteenth birthday, I fasted all day so that I could splurge
that night on beer. I chewed sugarless gum in place of meals. By
the time I returned from my driver's-education class, I was famished. I almost gave in when I saw the delectable birthday cake
my mom had bought for me and my twin sister: a light and flaky
white sheet cake with vanilla icing made from a dozen bars of
butter—the archenemy of any adolescent girl trying to maintain
her weedy, third-world figure, an enemy that happens to taste incredibly good in first-world baked goods. Yep, butter mixed with
sugar and flour can effectively throw a birthday bash right there
in your mouth, when all the taste buds who have been hibernat-
ing under the tongue, shy with social anxiety, come out to greet
the delicious ingredients and start chanting in unison: "Party . . .
party . . . party."

Alas. No party. Instead, I cut a piece and played with the cake
and icing with my fingers, bringing it to my nose and smelling it
like the sophisticated French rat, Remy, in *Ratatouille*. The rat said:
"Trust me, you want to eat this." The skeleton said: "Butter, dude.
We don't do butter." So I tried to engage my other senses, minus
hearing, to experience my birthday cake in the same way that celi-
bates make themselves believe they are experiencing sex when, in

fact, they are just getting licked under the chin by their mutt. In other words, a vivid imagination is required.

At my lowest weight, when I was a freshman in high school, I weighed 103 pounds, so thin I stopped menstruating. My body mass index (BMI) was 16, healthy being between 18.5 and 25; however, when I peered into the mirror, the girl looking back at me was a plump and pimply ballerina.

Of course it didn't help that my dance instructor encouraged us to be hollow-cheeked and scrawny. One afternoon she sized me up and down after I complained of a pulled muscle from running a few miles after ballet practice. She rolled her eyes, shook her head, and said, "Well, I guess you're not *that* fat," which, to my anorexic ears sounded like this: "You're obese." And yet, in comparison to the other gaunt girls in the class that didn't know what butter or sugar or flour were, she was right: I wasn't *that* fat.

Intense, studious girls in junior high often develop eating disorders in our culture because their bodies are something that they can control. These illnesses aren't about food any more than my childhood OCD was about rosaries. Like addictions, eating disorders are about practicing certain behaviors to get an intended result. When a young girl is able to consistently generate a result like loose pants, she gets hooked on that false sense of control.

Anorexia, especially, is fueled by the menacing combination of low self-esteem and perfectionism.

I can so relate to what Cherry Boone O'Neill wrote in her memoir, *Starving for Attention*:

> In my early years I equated my worth as a person with the level of my performance and I felt that the love and approval of other people would be conditional upon my perfection. Therefore, I expended every effort to be the best I could possibly be in any given area of endeavor, only

to repeatedly fall short of my goals and risk losing value in the eyes of others. Trying even harder, only to miss the mark again and again, resulted in compounded guilt and self-hatred.

My perfectionism at age fourteen was, quite literally, killing me.

I was president of my freshman class and was ranked second academically. I was also dancing almost every afternoon at the studio downtown.

All outward signs showed success. And yet I remember feeling as hollow as my cheeks.

According to J. Raymond DePaulo, Jr., MD, professor of psychiatry and director of the Affective Disorders Clinic at the Johns Hopkins University School of Medicine, young women diagnosed with eating disorders—anorexia nervosa, bulimia nervosa, and binge eating—have very high rates of depression, especially forms of chronic depression and manic depression.

I understand why Johns Hopkins combines its inpatient eating disorder clinic with its inpatient psychiatric unit at its hospital: poor body image is yet another face of depression. In some ways, it is depression's evil twin, because while they are stuck in the Black Hole, depressives face all kinds of eating predicaments—losing weight, gaining weight, or fluctuating between the two. And while a person is depressed, breaking free of any destructive behavior like an eating disorder is so very difficult.

Twenty years later, in 2006, when I was hospitalized in the psych unit at Johns Hopkins for severe depression, I roomed with an anorexic woman who looked like she belonged in a biology lab. Her spine was so pronounced that I could see each of the small bones in her lumbar vertebrae. The first night of my stay the nurses checked her vitals every two hours. I thought they should check them ever half-hour because I was truly unsure if she would make it that long. Her clothes could have fit Katherine's bigger dolls.

Getting my blood pressure taken one evening, I asked a veteran nurse which illness—an eating disorder or a mood disorder—is harder to overcome.

"An eating disorder, hands down," he said. "Because you have to eat to stay alive, and so it's always there. You are always confronting your behavior." Butter, flour, and friends are always at the table sprouting horns.

Depression has bullied me much more than an eating disorder, and I'd take anorexia or bulimia any day over the intense suicidal thoughts I experienced for eighteen months later in life. But before giving birth and whacking out my brain chemistry, I did get to enjoy several years symptom-free of depression. There were many days I didn't even think about my mood! But to this day the eating disorder is still there. At every meal.

In fact, I have endowed it with a voice and given it a name—ED, my first boyfriend, who gave me a scale for Valentine's Day with a gift certificate to Jenny Craig. Not really. "ED" is the initials of "eating disorder," which is why you probably shouldn't use it as a PIN to your grocery store credit card.

When Ed is around, my brain abandons all logic and thinks like this: If the Chinese government won't allow anyone with a BMI of over 40 to adopt their babies, then I should be less than half of that. Preferably 18 or under. Although, given that I take two kinds of antidepressants plus a mood stabilizer, I'm not in the running for a kid anyway.

This scoundrel Ed interprets compliments from my mom and other people like "You look good"—meaning "healthy and happy," not "skinny and shaking"—into fat alarms: *Alert! She is saying you've gained weight!* He delights in hearing things like "I'm concerned—you're getting too thin," because that means *Score! I'm on my way to looking emaciated!*

But if I know it's Ed who is talking, then he loses much of his power over me. My eating disorder is part of my larger problem: it's a cousin of depression residing in the obsessive-compulsive, perfectionist suburb of my mentally ill brain. Which means many of the techniques I apply to my mood disorder can help me tame Ed, as well. More on that later.

The Prison of Perfectionism

I have a magnet on my refrigerator that reads, "Jesus loves you, but everyone else thinks you're an asshole."

It's a gentle but effective reminder that on those days that I manage to tick off every person around me, God will still give me an invitation to his big bash in heaven if I say sorry and try harder tomorrow.

Perfectionism is like an untreated person with OCD who gets stuck analyzing a lady bug on a blade of grass—struggling to determine what shade of brown its dots are instead of appreciating the view of a spectacular rose garden she's in.

Like practically every other depressive I know, perfectionism can cripple my efforts to live freely and happily, not to mention plague me with writer's block. Left unattended, perfectionism will build a prison around me so that every shot at expressing myself is thwarted by the fear of not getting it right. Julia Cameron writes in *The Artist's Way*:

> Perfectionism is a refusal to let yourself move ahead. It is a loop—an obsessive, debilitating closed system that causes you to get stuck in the details of what you are writing or painting or making and to lose sight of the whole. Instead

of creating freely and allowing errors to reveal themselves later as insights, we often get mired in getting the details right. We correct our originality into a uniformity that lacks passion and spontaneity.

Writing Beyond Blue has been an important exercise for me to tackle my perfectionism. When your contract stipulates that you produce two to four posts a day, you can't afford to waste time trying to make each of them perfect. Besides, my editor, Holly, constantly reminds me to write from wherever *I am*, not from where *I want to be*, because the journey—full of backward steps—is what makes material real and most helpful to readers.

Sometimes I read through my archives and cringe at the awkwardness in my phrasing, the crude content of a post, especially when I compare myself with bestselling authors like Anne Lamott and Kathleen Norris. But then I try to let it go and get started on a new post because, as Anna Quindlen says, "perfection is static, even boring. Your unvarnished self is what is wanted."

Mistakes and all.

Chapter Three

Booze

The Quiet Car in My Very Loud Brain

In recovery circles, people tell newcomers that they belong if they can remember their first drink.

I don't.

But I remember my first buzz.

I was wearing an itsy-bitsy, teeny-weeny, pink polka-dot bikini that was falling off of my bony chest and hips because I was going for the emaciated Cambodian look. It was spring break of my freshman year in high school, and my family was vacationing in Siesta Key, Florida. A group of high-school guys invited my twin sister and me to a party. She drank a beer. I tried a wine cooler.

The next night I drank two strawberry daiquiris and I realized why alcohol was sometimes referred to as "spirits": with two drinks, my thoughts hushed. And in my busy and obsessive brain, that felt like a miracle. Enough booze allowed me to find the quiet car in the noisy, rush-hour Amtrak train of my mind. Liquor was twice as efficient at this task than meditative yoga. And it was so much more fun.

Booze replaced God as my best friend. No need for all those no-venas and rosaries, because with a shot of vodka in me I instantly felt prettier, smarter, and gosh darn it, people seemed to like me!

Liquor became a kind of babysitter for my brain, handling all the obnoxious commotion so that I, like a new mom of a colicky baby, could get away and relax.

Alcohol paved the path to my freedom.

The setup for my addiction was ideal. By the time I was fifteen and a sophomore in high school, my dad lived in an elegant brick Tudor home a few miles away from the childhood house where my sisters and I lived with our mom. In his spacious basement, my dad stocked three closets full of Absolut Vodka. He wasn't exactly a sloppy drunk—he was one of the top manufacturer's sales representatives in the automobile industry for the Indiana, Ohio, and Kentucky region and, in addition, had started and operated a tool-and-die company with three other men—but I never saw him without a martini in his hand in the evening. On the Monday night dinners where my sisters, my dad, and I would order takeout Chinese or a pizza from his house, I'd wander down to the basement and steal a few bottles. He had so many that pilfering a few bottles a week was like tossing a few pieces of luggage off the *Titanic*.

I hid some liquor underneath my bed and buried a few bottles in a bush in the backyard. To get a head start on my buzz most Friday and Saturday evenings, I'd pour a few ounces of vodka into my diet Coke—a kind of pre-cocktail cocktail that made the mascara easier to apply. As my tolerance increased, so too did the amount of vodka in my pre-cocktail cocktail. But that was okay because I looked just like my older sisters, which meant I could borrow their driver's licenses to buy beer for the parties.

But like all destructive behaviors that keep you from going inward and doing the hard work, booze turned on me. The stuff to which I attributed my social grace, beauty, and intelligence was nothing but a backstabber that ultimately brought me to a place where I cried uncle and asked God to take over.

I hit bottom a few times. And each time hurt more than the previous one.

The evening of St. Patrick's Day during my junior year in high school, I downed a half-dozen shots of Everclear, a highly flammable brand of ethanol with a concentration of up to 95 percent alcohol, or 190 proof. And I chased those down with some green beer.

The parents of my friend Sue were throwing a party like they did every year. Both Sue and her brother, a freshman at the University of Dayton, invited friends over to cocktail downstairs in the basement while their folks hosted happy hour upstairs. Then everyone under twenty-one headed to the bars by the university, in the off-campus housing section called the "ghetto."

That's where my memory ends: in a crowded sedan, where ten people were on top of each other in the car. In my green miniskirt, I was sitting on the lap of a friend of Sue's brother.

My next memory was waking up in some ghetto house full of beer cans, empty bottles, cigarette butts and roaches (marijuana butts). Later I saw the blood stains on my white underwear.

My first four thoughts in their proper order:

I was raped.

I could be pregnant.

I can't have an abortion.

My life is over.

I begged Sue to investigate. A month later she reported that there was absolutely no foul play. And because I didn't want to believe differently, I tried to forget it ever happened.

I stayed away from booze for a good two months after that. But the noise in my head got so loud; the voices were obnoxious. I missed the quiet car. So I began stealing vodka from my dad again. A few months passed and I woke up in the same dreadful place—on the disgusting floor of a UD ghetto house.

This time I couldn't walk.

While intoxicated, I apparently judged that I had supernatural flying abilities because I jumped out of a two-story house. I landed on my heels, which was better than on my back. But they were so badly bruised from the clumsy stunt that I had to wobble around on my tiptoes for three months. This happened in August, so I went into my senior year walking like Back-to-School Barbie and was suspended again from the high-school drill team, a dance squad of sixty girls who dressed like the Dallas Cowgirls but kicked like the Rockettes. The first time I was booted off of this kick line was when I got busted for packing vodka in my band-camp luggage. The way I saw it, after jumping off ladders into splits for eight hours in the hot sun for an entire week, you sure as heck deserved a nightcap.

You would think those two events alone would be enough to make me quit drinking forever. But I still needed proof the stuff was responsible for all these bad things that happened. So I added to my mortified moments the mornings I woke up in between trash cans on the lawn of a classmate, in a friend's closet—my mom subsequently told me that my dad used to pass out in closets, too, so I guess it runs in the family—or on a couch of a friend of a friend, with his concerned father peering over me as if he were gauging whether or not I was breathing.

My disease progressed to the point where almost every time I drank I passed out. I dreaded the phone call the next day when I'd have to ask a friend: "What happened?"

One day senior year, my twin sister, Trish, turned around to me in homeroom and simply said, "You need to cool it."

Her five words spoke more directly to me than any educational pamphlet about alcoholism could: "If you said yes to at least five of the above questions, *congrats!* You're in for a lifetime of sparkling water with lime."

Wait. Who was telling me how to behave? Trish, who I suspected had broken all ten commandments by the time she got her period and had accumulated more demerits than my two other sisters and me combined, was telling *me* to chill out? The one who moved in with my dad the fall of our junior year in high school because she couldn't abide by my mom's rules?

Of course, she was right.

And I know why she said what she did.

A few weeks prior to her suggestions for behavioral modification, she told me to ask Jim, a good friend of her boyfriend's (Bill) to the senior year turn-about dance—the chicks ask the boys—so that we could go together.

My only memories of that night are slamming beers and getting so high at Bill's place that we skipped the dance and instead drove, intoxicated and high, to a nice Italian restaurant. We were laughing hysterically and behaving so obnoxiously that there were complaints from other tables. I remember eating my pasta dish with my fingers and spilling the marinara sauce all over my lavender dress. Later, when we returned to Bill's place, Bill and Trish took off somewhere, leaving me alone with my date. I tried to kiss him, but he turned his cheek.

I disgusted him.

Liquor had lost its redemptive powers.

W hat eventually got me sober was a concept called *integrity.*

I was losing it fast.

Imagine a Catholic version of Miley Cyrus / Hannah Montana. By day I coordinated liturgies for school, wrote daily prayers that I read over the intercom, and was teacher's pet in religion class. By night, I was a heavy partier who would lie, steal, and cheat to get her booze.

I remember earning an award for outstanding community service during my senior year. The principal of Archbishop Alter High School personally drove me downtown for the ceremony, where other seniors from different schools would also be awarded. My mom was away that week, so a friend was staying with me. We bought a keg and got drunk every night.

The morning of the award, I woke up with a nasty hangover, reeking of beer and cigarettes. I threw on my wrinkled school uniform, chewed spearmint gum, and sprayed perfume all over me, but I still smelled like a keg part when I climbed into the principal's car. Several news stations were there, of course, because they always are when you're hung over and want to hide.

That night I sat on the kitchen floor with my friend Carolyn, holding a large plastic cup of beer from the keg, smoking a cigarette, as I enjoyed a nice buzz.

Then the news came on, and there I was on the TV, getting my award. The phone rang. It was my uncle. He congratulated me on the award.

"Thanks," I said, feeling as though I was shoving my lover into the closet as my husband unexpectedly walked in. Magnificent buzz and all, I felt like the most insincere, inauthentic person in all of Dayton, Ohio. I wished that I could give my award to a deserving person, because I was sure that I was headed for hell. And it had nothing to do with not saying enough rosaries.

I don't know how, exactly, I was able to turn around at that point. Not to sound like one of those football players who pontificates about what God has done in his life on national TV while his dad holds the John 3:16 sign over his head, but I think most of my getting sober was God's work. All I did was listen to the angel, a special high school teacher, that he sent my way.

She spotted the mammoth red flags: my slurring my words over the intercom as I said the morning prayer, my stumbling cross-eyed into the auditorium at the Homecoming dance, my downing the church wine after class liturgies. So she sat me down on the stairs of the main entrance to the school for a chat.

"What's going on?" she asked me, point-blank, no fillers.

"Nothing," I almost replied. Further confessions might mean more demerits. But there was something in the way she inquired that made me think our talk might change my life.

Looking back now, I was right.

"This isn't you," she said. "You can be so much more."

I would have blown off her words had they not articulated the agonizing rip I felt inside me. On the one hand, booze was a divine anesthesia. It removed so much of my pain. It allowed me to tolerate myself. It numbed me to all the damn neuroses inside my brain that I had been fighting since the beginning. In so many ways, it was the means to paradise, the end of my struggling.

Yet alcohol had also begun to play me as its fool: dressing me up like a celebrity and feeding me feel-good lies, only to rip off my clothes at the last moment and have me stand on the stage naked before my audience. My apologies were worthless after a while because I uttered them so often to family and friends. "Yeah, yeah, yeah, you drank too much . . . and that's why you did it. Tell me something new," they'd say. I lost credibility with all the people closest to me because drunken behavior often kept me from following through on my promises: "Sure. I'll meet you there at nine—unless I'm drunk before then." Even if I was sincere in saying sorry, my girlfriends were right to predict the same type of irresponsibility a week later.

I remember one day my senior year looking into the bathroom mirror at school and feeling absolute disgust at who I had become. I just sat there, in front of the mirror, and couldn't stop crying. It was as if someone had cast a spell on me. I didn't want to do the things that I was doing, and I was cognizant of the spell. But I hadn't a clue as to how to break it. And that was the only way to regain control of my actions.

So I did what my mom always did when she needed direction: I prayed a novena to St. Therese.

On the fifth day of my novena, the florist came to the door with three red roses for me from a certain angel who had me in class. The card said this:

Just remember, in the winter
Far beneath the bitter snows
Lies the seed that with the sun's love
In the spring, becomes the rose.

I decided, then and there, that I was going to venture out of my comfort zone, that I no longer needed liquor to coat my nerves or quiet my mind, that I'd find another way to peace. I wasn't sure about all the details in the contract I was signing, but somewhere, somehow, those roses gave me the courage to say Amen. Just like that quote from Dag Hammarskjold:

I don't know Who—or what—put the question, I don't know when it was put. I don't even remember answering. But at some moment I did answer Yes to Someone—or Something—and from that hour I was certain that existence is meaningful and that, therefore, my life, in self-surrender, had a goal.

11 Ways You Know You're an Addict

1. You can recite the Serenity Prayer in three different languages.
2. Abstinence is easier than moderation.
3. New Year's Day is always the first day of a new life that ends approximately twenty-four hours later.
4. Denial ain't just a river in Egypt. It's also the city water with which you wash your hair.
5. You choose friends with habits that make yours look good.
6. When you look up the term *dysfunctional* in the dictionary, you find a portrait of your family of origin.
7. You attend so many support groups that you get confused how to introduce yourself: *Hi, I'm Therese and I'm a . . . wait . . . um . . . oh . . . child of an alcoholic!*
8. You accidentally feed your sobriety chip to a vending machine.
9. Dopamine is your favorite hormone, which unfortunately robs your brain of logic and common sense.
10. You never unpack from your guilt trip because with all your frequent-flyer miles, every day is a vacation.
11. You have the potential to do great things in this world.

Chapter Four

It's Depression

Naming the Pain

Th only devils in the world are those running in our own hearts," wrote Mahatma Gandhi. "That is where the battle should be fought." Personally, I'd toss in a few personalities like Hitler and Saddam Hussein. But I agree that the heart is our primary war zone.

As I said in the last chapter, I gave up booze two months before graduating from high school. Now think about every college freshman you know, and read that sentence again. Meaning this: I chose the worst possible time to jump on the sobriety wagon that is available to drunks.

I hopped on without a clue as to where it was going. So with expectations of a fun and relaxing ride, I was a bit taken aback when the driver told everyone to get out and start shoveling horse crap. Yep, while most American college freshmen prepared to rebel like Lindsay Lohan with their first dose of freedom, I hunkered down with my coffee and Marlboro Lights and wondered if there was anyone I could hang out with in the library besides the janitor.

Moreover, by the time I was assigned a peer group for freshman orientation at Saint Mary's College in South Bend, I had finally stopped running from the enemy—alcoholism, OCD, and disordered eating—so it was there, on that exquisite campus that I confronted the deep, raw anguish lurking behind all of them.

The pain, it turned out, had a name: *depression*.

Luckily for me I had a brave, compassionate emissary who could begin to translate what, exactly, I needed to do to tame the demon that raged within me. Nancy, my college therapist, along with a few of my professors, fought alongside me during this most critical crusade within my soul.

I made an appointment with Nancy the first week of school to inquire about support-group meetings in the area. Suspecting there was more to my struggle than staying sober, she politely invited me back. And back. And back. And back. Until I graduated, when the school no longer funded my visits.

Nancy helped me to separate my fear from my conscious self, so that I could observe the panic from a few different angles, call it a jerk, draw a picture of it to send home, and then put it on a leash and enroll it in obedience class. That way I became its master, not vice versa. With one ordinary question, she could move me from a place of confusion to clarity. Language led to understanding, and understanding led to healing. So by articulating my ugly thoughts for the first time, I could begin to do something about them.

She was the first one to drop the D word. Which made me run. To my dorm room, where I hid.

There I'd bury my head in the writings of the Carmelite saints Teresa of Avila and Therese of Lisieux. Because their words made sense of my suffering. They had experienced their own inner torment and said it served a higher purpose. According to these two heroes, if I kept talking to God, in time I might reach a place of stillness and peace, a mountaintop of ecstasy, or perfect union with God.

In her second chapter of the classic *Interior Castle*, Teresa of Avila wrote:

I have just been wondering if my God could be described as the fire in a lighted brazier, from which some spark will fly out and touch the soul, in such a way that it will be able to feel the burning heat of the fire; but, as the fire is not hot enough to burn it up, and the experience is very delectable, the soul continues to feel that pain and the mere touch suffices to produce that effect in it.

And Therese of Lisieux—the Little Flower—wrote:

Life is often irksome and bitter; it is hard to begin a laborious day, above all when Jesus hides Himself from us. What is this tender Friend doing? Does He not then see our anguish, the load that oppresses us; where is He? Why does He not come to console us? Ah, fear not . . . He is there, quite near! He is watching us.

God wants me to suffer, I'd think. *He's preparing me for something important, something that I will come to understand in time. It is a privilege to cry. It means I'm among his special children.*
I remember walking the snowy paths of Saint Mary's charming campus feeling so alone. And scared. And confused. I was often tempted to drive to the liquor store, buy a few bottles of vodka, and enjoy some screwdrivers and Marlboro Lights in my dorm room. Instead I'd sit Indian style on the floor of the chapel in Holy Cross Hall. I would light a candle and stare into its flame for an hour or more.

I assumed that God heard me better if I stuck my face in a hot glowing body of fire. Doesn't everyone? I mean, really, look at all the popular candle shops these days. Lighting a candle comforted and soothed me. The scarlet blaze generated a feeling of promise, of fierce tenacity, that whispered: *You're not off the hook yet. Hang in there.*

I would pray for a tiny crumb of hope, a beginning of light, or a dawn. I prayed to feel good and right, though I didn't really know what that was.

In our sessions, I told Nancy all about my aunt Mary Lou, how I feared that I was like her: because if I was, my life would become as miserable as hers, and it would end tragically, in a garage full of carbon monoxide.

During one session, Nancy was firmer than usual.

"Coping your way through life is not a way to live, Therese," she said. "If you just admit to depression, or to a mood disorder, then I can help get you the treatment you need, and your life can be better."

I didn't see an easier life. I saw Mary Lou's face.

I ran to my dorm room and called my mom.

"Mom, I'm not like Mary Lou, right? You told me I wasn't like Mary Lou!"

"You're not like Mary Lou," she told me. "You're not."

My mom and Nancy spoke on the phone. During our next session Nancy looked me straight in the eyes and asked me, "Why is it so important that you not be like your aunt Mary Lou?"

She paused for what seemed like a semester and confronted me with the truth.

"I think both you and your mother are in denial," she said, which sent me again to my room.

It was a beautiful spring day toward the end of April, my sophomore year. There was a school picnic set up right outside my dorm. I could smell burgers and hear the DJ. I opened my small window to feel the breeze and hear the music.

A friend knocked on the door.

"Are you going?" she asked, peeking inside.

"No. I'm sick," I responded.

Rather, I'm ill, I told myself. *I'm mentally ill . . . I'm mentally ill . . . I'm mentally ill.* I repeated those words like a mantra.

I'm a freak. I'm a total freak, I thought. *Just like Mary Lou. This is exactly when her nightmare started . . . when she was twenty. I'm going to end up dead in a garage somewhere.* I curled up in a fetal position on my bed, like an infant terrified of her new world, and I cried all night.

By the winter of my freshman year, Nancy strongly suggested that I try some antidepressants, but I was adamantly opposed.

Because that would have been a cop-out.

"Strong people don't take antidepressants" was the very clear message I heard at church, from my friends and family, and especially in sobriety circles.

When I told my AA sponsor that my therapist wanted to start me on some medicine, she warned me: "Those happy pills will compromise your sobriety."

Today I realize the recovery cultures of addiction and mental illness clash. Like the Church of Scientology and neurobiology. Like Tom Cruise and common sense. Because complaining is considered whining to most twelve-steppers—"poor me, poor me, pour me a drink"—but as a smart disclosure of symptoms to mental-health professionals. Because many recovering alcoholics and drug addicts are not educated about mental illness, a lot of bad advice is doled out at meetings and/or social hours. With the best of intentions, of course. But dangerous all the same.

I was intimidated by the AA old-timers and afraid to think any differently from them, fearing that if I listened to my gut, I would become one of those people who were "too smart" for the program and relapsed continuously. Who was I to question the direction and counsel given by the guys who had been sober over a quarter of a century? *They want to die, too. They just don't talk about it,* I surmised. *And neither will I.*

Back then I wish I would have known about the research done by people like Ken Duckworth, MD, the medical director for the National Alliance on Mental Illness and an assistant professor at Harvard University Medical School. I interviewed him last year for Beyond Blue, and here's what he said:

> In the substance abuse culture, the person is generally viewed as the agent of the problem, and they are held accountable and have consequences for their relapses. In the mental illness culture, the person is often viewed not as the agent of the problem, but as the victim of their illness. We tend to hold people a little less accountable for biochemical processes. . . .
>
> You can see this dichotomy. And when I work with families dealing with both conditions, my heart really goes out to them because in the AA world, and in the substance abuse culture, they are encouraged to have the person hit bottom and be accountable, but that's not the case in the mental health world.

For the first three years of my sobriety in college, my struggle consisted not so much in fighting the craving for alcohol like most of the young people in the support groups I knew, but in dealing with the obsessive thoughts regarding alcohol. I couldn't figure out what to do with this question of whether or not I was an alcoholic.

While I was at Saint Mary's, I attended three or more meetings a week, where I would often say something like, "Hi, I'm Therese and I don't like what happens to me when I drink alcohol," because I just couldn't utter the word *alcoholic* two words after the word *I*.

I was afraid of labels. I hated them.

I stumbled and stalled at step one—accepting that I was powerless over alcohol—unable to progress to step two: coming to believe in a power greater than ourselves—which I was cool with. *What makes someone an alcoholic?* I wondered. *Am I really allergic to the stuff? What would happen if I went to the Linebacker bar with some friends and got smashed?* Over and over and over again, these questions haunted me.

Toward the end of my junior year, I attended a meeting devoted to the first step.

"Without the first step, without accepting the fact that you are powerless over alcohol, you may as well give up the program," said one guy.

"It's the foundation," said another.

They're right, I thought. *If I can't say with certainty that I am powerless over booze, then I'm never going to be able to get to step two and make peace with this whole sobriety thing. This doubt will always be there, keeping me from living freely and happily. It's just a matter of time before I get drunk. So I may as well guzzle down some beers right now.*

I drove my Ford Taurus up to the Indiana-Michigan state line from South Bend. It was a Sunday night and Indiana was dry on the Lord's Day. I bought a six-pack of Coors Light, drove back to Saint Mary's College, parked the car in the student lot, and knocked back the cans. Then I waited to see what would happen—if my complexion would turn green, if my fingernails would start to curl—some tangible sign that I was, in fact, allergic to these types of beverages.

The next day I confessed to Nancy what I had done, and how I wanted to end my life because I was so disgusted with myself. *How could I have done something so stupid? Ruin three years of sobriety? And so close to my three-year chip?*

"But I can't do that damn first step!" I explained to her, panicking. "And if I can't do the first step, I can't move forward."

"Therese," she said very calmly, "you just told me that you are ready to end your life because you are so obsessed with this question and your struggle with alcohol. I'd say, then, that you are powerless over it. If you can't say that you are powerless over alcohol itself, then say you are powerless over your obsession with alcohol."

Oh. Now that made sense. Because there were times when I drank that I could stop after two. I didn't always pass out in a friend's coat closet or wake up between two trash cans on a neighbor's lawn. But the obsession about alcohol—well, yeah, that drove me absolutely crazy.

Friends, hearing that liquor and I were a pair again, invited me to parties that I wanted to attend in the worst way. After all, I deserved to taste the college experience after living three years as a cloistered nun. With one foot in the Linebacker bar and the other in the convent, I was more confused than ever. And the upheaval was poison to my mind and soul, my body and spirit.

Finally I walked to the gazebo in back of Our Lady of Loretto Church, my favorite spot on the campus of Saint Mary's and the place where Eric proposed to me three years later. I looked over the St. Joseph's River like I had done so many times after running around the campus.

"God," I pleaded, "I can't hold on to this anymore. I can't say for sure whether or not I'm an alcoholic, but I want peace more than anything. And it appears that when I drink bad things happen to me. Is that enough to make the first step? I want so badly to please you and to do what is right, but I can't take these obsessions anymore. So if you take this urge from me—all of my preoccupation with booze—then I will do my best to stay sober and do your will. . . . In other words, God, I give this to you. Please take it."

I lifted my arms above me, and looked down at the current

in the river. And I felt peace. So much peace. A peace about this whole alcoholism issue that I hadn't felt since before I tasted my first wine cooler and found the quiet car in the crazy Amtrak train of my brain.

I haven't had a drink since.

I'm very indebted to those meetings early on in my recovery. Getting sober was the first step to where I am today, and meetings helped me stay sober. But my real breakthrough came with educating myself about mental illness: that antidepressants are *not* happy pills, that they won't compromise sobriety, and that they, in fact, will make sobriety better, because I will start to live and not just cope.

Nancy approached her discipline much like a lawyer or a detective or maybe the Pink Panther. She delved into the details of my earlier life—obtained all the appropriate test results and feedback she could find—and then consolidated the information to arrive at a proper diagnosis. Or four: OCD, eating disorder, generalized anxiety disorder, and major depression. Then she pleaded her case, which was, of course, the hard part.

For example, I had totally forgotten about a psychological/aptitude/intelligence test my mom made me do as a disciplinary action for my alcohol abuse. Although she didn't think I was an alcoholic—get real, I was only seventeen—she didn't like my bizarre behavior as it related to liquids drunk from a bottle. To figure out what was going on inside her teenager's noggin, she made me attend six sessions that combined therapy and aptitude assessment with a flair of Tony Robbins's motivational punch: *you're good enough, you're smart enough, gosh darn it, why do you keep on getting smashed and messing up?* In the assessment, the psychologist wrote this:

It was determined that this student is under a lot of stress. We discussed stress management and other ways to cope other than alcohol use. As you can see from her . . . profile, she has a pattern that would suggest lots of frustration and disability with memory function, auditory and visual concentration, and verbal expression. Because she was not a poor student no learning disability intervention was sought but she certainly has a unique, fragile learning style.

That piece of evidence, and others like it that she would find, helped her case: that my affliction wasn't merely a dark night of the soul that would eventually land in light—that there were some very real biochemical abnormalities that could be treated with meds.

Nancy pieced together clues from my past—learning difficulties, intrusive thoughts, anxiety, perfectionism—in order to know how best to guide me toward recovery. Each week she would send me home with a new handout: on how to improve concentration or resolve test anxiety, or a chapter from *The Anxiety and Phobia Workbook* by Edmund J. Bourne, PhD.

She strongly encouraged me to read two books that forever changed the way I viewed my painful past and framed my present struggle: *The Boy Who Couldn't Stop Washing: The Experience and Treatment of Obsessive-Compulsive Disorder* by Judith L. Rapoport, MD, and Colette Dowling's *You Mean I Don't Have to Feel This Way? New Help for Depression, Anxiety, and Addiction.*

While reading through Rapoport's book, I immediately recalled all the weird stuff I did and thought as a young girl: the anxiety about confession—if I forgot to list all twenty-seven sins, something horrible would happen to either me or the priest who heard my confession; the compulsion to touch something like a Marian medal over and over again as I said to myself "Twin Powers, acti-vate!"; hoarding letters, old corsages, movie-ticket stubs, and other keepsakes under my bed; being absolutely terrified of throwing things away; flapping my arms when I got excited, which went over real well at the Homecoming dance; obsessing about Mary Lou and whether or not I was crazy; obsessing about whether or not my tongue was in the right place when I swallowed; checking my math homework over and over and over again; and being petrified of hell, of the devil, and of dying.

I cried when I read Rapoport's description of scrupulosity, in the chapter where she tells the stories of some of her clients, like Sally, a sixth grader preparing for her Confirmation:

> A few weeks before the big day [Sally] started having crying spells, couldn't sleep, and lost ten pounds. It all began suddenly, when Sally was doing a class punishment assignment. She thought that she wasn't doing it prop-erly, that she was "sinning." I'm always doing something wrong, she felt. The feeling stayed with her.
>
> Each day her symptoms became more intense. "If I touch the table, I'm really offending God," she whispered. She folded her arms and withdrew into deep thought. Sally was terror-struck that she might have offended God by touching her hands. Did that mean that she was strik-ing God? She wondered, retreating further into herself.

And in the pages of *You Mean I Don't Have to Feel This Way?* I found true relief and enough research to convince me that antidepressants were not a cop-out and that my depression was a very real and se-rious illness. Dowling spoke directly to me and my skepticism in chapter seven: "When Sobriety Is Not Enough."

Early in that chapter she quotes Daniel Goleman, then a science writer for the *New York Times*:

> For several years, scientists have suspected that at least some drug addicts suffer imbalances in brain chemistry that made them vulnerable to depression, anxiety or intense restlessness. For such people, addiction becomes a kind of self-medication in which drugs correct the chemical imbalance and bring a sort of relief.

Dowling goes on to say that scientists believe identifying an underlying psychiatric disorder and intervening medically will help treat the addiction as well as the disorder. After reading the following paragraph I finally understood why I craved booze from the time I experienced my first buzz, and what that had to do with the biological underpinnings of my depression:

> Scientists think that in predisposed humans the production of endorphins and enkephalins in the brain is abnormally low from birth. Low levels of these mood-regulating chemicals result in anxiety and a feeling of need that is extremely uncomfortable. It is this bad feeling that makes people susceptible to the brief mood-lifts provided by drinking and drug taking. They are not really looking for euphoria. What they long for, what their bodies are trying to achieve, is the state of chemical balance that those of us enjoy who are fortunate to have enough neurotransmitters in the first place.

Once every word in Dowling's book was underlined with three different highlighters and I'd memorized the journal abstracts of five studies confirming the biological basis of my depression, I finally gave Nancy the green light to experiment with some antidepressants.

After three tries, we stumbled upon the odd combination of Prozac and Zoloft, both selective serotonin reuptake inhibitors (SSRIs). Sobriety became much easier. I no longer spent hours obsessing about whether or not I was an alcoholic and if I had done the first step perfectly. I was able to get through Cicero and Tolstoy without crying at the end of every page, calling myself a stupid idiot, plus a filler or two. And, best of all, by finding the right psychopharmaceutical cocktail, I was able to do the cognitive work in therapy that I was unable to do before: to sort out my childhood anxiety and to identify distorted thinking that led to self-hatred.

Some people need only to attend a weekly 12-step meeting, or roam the self-help section at Borders, or sit down for a cappuccino with a friend to feel good.

I'm high-maintenance.

I need my daily pills, even as I hate taking them. And I'm not graduating from talk therapy anytime soon. Those are the two primary pillars of my mental-health program for the same reasons Kay Redfield Jamison explains in her memoir, *An Unquiet Mind*:

> At this point in my existence, I cannot imagine leading a normal life without both taking lithium and having had the benefits of psychotherapy. Lithium prevents my seductive but disastrous highs, diminishes my depressions, clears out the wool and webbing from my disordered thinking, slows me down, gentles me out, keeps me from ruining my career and relationships, keeps me out of a hospital, alive, and makes psychotherapy possible. But, ineffably, psychotherapy heals. It makes some sense of the confusion, reins in the terrifying thoughts and feelings,

returns some control and hope and possibility of learning from it all. Pills cannot, do not, ease one back into reality; they only bring one back headlong, careening, and faster than can be endured at times. Psychotherapy is a sanctuary; it is a battleground; it is a place I have been psychotic, neurotic, elated, confused, and despairing beyond belief. But, always, it is where I have believed—or have learned to believe—that I might someday be able to contend with all of this. . . .

No pill can help me deal with the problem of not wanting to take pills; likewise, no amount of psychotherapy alone can prevent my manias and depressions. I need both. It is an odd thing, owing life to pills, one's own quirks and tenacities, and this unique, strange, and ultimately profound relationship called psychotherapy.

SANITY BREAK

Love the Questions

Have patience with everything unresolved in your heart
and try to love the questions themselves. . . . Don't search
for the answers, which could not be given to you now,
because you would not be able to live them. And the point
is to live everything. Live the questions now. Perhaps then,
someday far in the future, you will gradually, without even
noticing it, live your way into the answer.

—*Rainer Marie Rilke*

Chapter Five

From the Maternity Ward to the Psych Ward

Four Simple Steps

Iknow it seems crazy to live your life according to signs from the universe, or, in my Catholic world, miracles and saintly intercessions. But the fact that I met Eric on the feast day of St. Therese makes me think that God somehow sanctioned our marriage and that Eric and I were meant for each other.

Just a few months after graduating from the University of Notre Dame with a master's degree in theology, I moved to Chicago to work as an editor for a magazine that Eric would later call *US Satan* because my boss hated me and some of my coworkers mocked me like we were all in the sixth grade again. A few weeks into the job, a friend from Saint Mary's came to visit and wanted to introduce me to a guy she knew in Chicago with a similar sense of humor to mine.

That guy was Eric, and she was right. I had never laughed so hard in one night as I did the evening we met. A year later, also on the feast day of St. Therese, he asked me to marry him at the same gazebo on the campus of Saint Mary's where I had begged God to take away my obsession with alcohol.

Humor has always been a strong antidote to my depression. The laughter that Eric brought into my life, not to mention the friendship and love, went a long way in helping me to achieve an emotional stability for the ten years following my graduation from college. I kept taking the cocktail—Prozac and Zoloft—that I was first prescribed at Saint Mary's, and I continued to practice all the other steps in my mental-health program: exercise, healthy diet, sobriety, prayer, friendship, yada yada yada. That was enough to ground me. Based on those ten years, I have a better idea of what normal people feel like. And it was wonderful.

However, nothing disrupts a woman's biochemistry like conceiving, carrying, and giving birth to a baby. So, for me, the walk from the maternity ward to the psych ward was a short one, involving four simple steps.

Step One. Swap a stimulating career as a freelance writer and editor, where you solicit lots of warm fuzzies and positive feedback on a daily basis, with one (i.e., motherhood) in which you feel as defective as a razor missing a blade. And that's without taking into consideration the loneliness, desperation, and confusion thrown in with your new job.

Step Two. Exchange a schedule of eight to nine hours of consistent sleep a night for a five-year period, in which a little person yells at you every three to four hours, just to make sure you never completely doze off. Does the anxious boy with chronic ear infections, gastrointestinal distress, nighttime terrors, and leg cramps ever take what other moms refer to as "naps"? Of course not. He doesn't need sleep. What irony! An adult who absolutely requires nine hours of sleep to function—or at least to control all the profanities that slip out when she's tired—giving birth to an insomniac!

Step Three. Invite the bleeding inner child to exit the uterus with the newborn, so that with every insecurity a new mom feels, that damn inner child screams "Issue! Issue! Issue! I think I found an issue!" as if it's trying to win the blue ribbon in the Issue Finding Contest, and the kid yells this in the same high-pitched squeal that the newborn makes in the middle of the night because, remember, he doesn't need sleep.

Step Four. Bring on a biochemical, hormonal, and neurological Armageddon of the brain that delivers a person to the land of hysteria, which borders the land of delusions and psychosis.

Let's go over these a little.

Crossing Over: Help, I'm Stuck!

I know that Jackie Onassis meant no harm when she wrote, "If you bungle raising your children, I don't think whatever else you do well matters very much." However, that line has haunted me whenever I receive feedback that makes me think I just wasn't cut out for the job.

Many stay-at-home moms thoroughly enjoy making crafts, compiling scrapbooks, and assembling puzzles. Some thrive at baking those reindeer cookies—where you use pretzels for antlers and red M&M's for noses—and decorating their homes with alphabetically arranged objects that they can point to, enunciating with perfect phonics what, indeed, the objects are: Cup! Apple! Banana (that's a hard one)!

I hate all of these activities.

And they hate me.

There is some nasty, toxic energy—possibly remnants of a constipated feng shui—going down between crafts, or all forms of domestication, and me.

An example:

For David's first Valentine's Day party at preschool I forgot to buy valentines, of course, so I frantically cut out eight hearts, one for each kid in his class, from my stack of scrap paper before we left the house. With a pink highlighter, I quickly scribbled on them "Happy Valentine's Day! From David."

"I didn't know you were a religion major," one of the moms said to me after I dispersed the sorry-looking hearts to the kids. How did she find out? My résumé was on the other side. So much for trying to save the earth!

That's the cute version of the story about a woman who used to get most of her self-esteem from professional success plunging into stay-at-home-motherhood cold turkey only to feel that she mucked it up at every turn; a tale about a chick who knew herself well enough to guess that the restlessness she would encounter by staying home would burden her less than the guilt that she would feel if she continued to work full-time, and made the decision based on that guilt equation; an account of a mom who was tormented by the voices of wise, elder moms whispering in her ear: "You won't regret the decision to stay home," "They are only this young once," "You'll be so glad you were there for their firsts," "It all goes by so quickly," and "There really is nothing so important."

My biggest flop—a story that landed our family on the front page of the *Annapolis Capital*—almost involved a fatality. The two-year-old boy under my care could have easily died had his guardian angel not been eating sushi on the edge of the city dock in Annapolis, where the Spa Creek of the Chesapeake Bay meets the quaint downtown shops.

A fellow preschool mom that I didn't know all that well asked if I'd take her two-and-a-half-year-old, Will, for an hour or two one February afternoon. Everything ran smoothly—David, Will, my new baby Katherine, and I ate lunch at my favorite restaurant downtown and then fed the ducks—until David pushed Will into the fifteen inches of frigid water. Because I had Katherine strapped to me in a Baby Bjorn, I could do nothing but scream as I tried frantically to unsnap the thing.

The kind gentleman eating California rolls at the dock dove in after Will and rescued him with the perfect timing of an *ER* episode. Although little Will had to climb aboard the ambulance (or "the cool truck," as David described it) and be examined at the hospital—with tubes in his ears, he wasn't supposed to be submerged in any water, let alone the polluted city dock—everything was fine in the end. But if the city were awarding a Mortified Mom Prize to the most humiliated mom in the community, I certainly would have claimed it. Moreover, the traumatic event confirmed for me what I had feared all along: that I wasn't mom material, and that I had grossly erred in thinking that I could be a suitable mother to anyone.

Country Motherhood: A Lonely and Exhausting Place

In her book of honest essays, *Mother Shock*, Andrea Buchanan compares the first year of motherhood to the culture shock you feel when you've just moved to a foreign country. She writes:

> This is what it feels like for many of us when we become mothers: we find we have entered into a strange new world with a language, culture, time zone, and set of customs all its own. Until we become acclimated to this new, seemingly unfathomable territory, we exist in a state of culture shock.

What was most difficult for me those first years of motherhood was the brutal combination of sleep deprivation and isolation. For a person prone to anxiety and depression, one of these alone is enough to trigger a full-blown depressive episode. Together, an ugly mental condition is virtually guaranteed.

David was not an easy baby. Or toddler. Or preschooler.

Like mine, David's anxiety has been there from before he was yanked out of my uterus in an emergency C-section. First it manifested itself as colic and gas. I couldn't calm the wee baby down. Then chronic ear and sinus infections had him crying out in pain every two hours through the night. After he got tubes and his adenoids were removed, we arrived at night terrors. And then the consistent leg cramps at night.

As I said a few pages back, for the first five years of his life, he didn't sleep for more than three or four hours at night. And he didn't nap.

"Well, that's because you didn't train him to sleep," the moms with perfectly sleeping babies would tell me. One of them suggested the "5-10-15 method": You go in after five minutes of screaming and gently pat him. Then you go in at 10 minutes and again console him. And by fifteen minutes? He's sound asleep!

In our house it was the "5 minutes, 10 minutes, 7 hours" strategy. I restrained myself from going into his room to comfort him after hours and hours of crying because I was convinced that everyone else knew better than I did when they said: "Stick with it. Don't give in. It's best for both of you. You have to set some boundaries now, from the start." In retrospect, knowing about David's two flaming red ears and sinus problems, I lament my poor judgment and shake my head at how easily I yielded my maternal instinct to people who didn't know any better than I did. They just thought they did. And I believed them.

After a few years of waking every three or four hours through the night, I was bait for a major depressive episode. Physiologically, sleep disruption messes with circadian rhythms, the twenty-four-hour clock system wired into our brain that governs fluctuations in body temperature and the secretion of several hormones. While there has always been some data to suggest that sleep deprivation may increase a mother's vulnerability to depression, some experts today claim that chronic sleep deprivation can, in fact, *cause* post-partum depression.

Not only did I wear pitch-black circles under my eyes after David was born, but I was without much company or support. Eric was devoted and faithful, as always, but he didn't lactate, so he could help only to a certain extent. Plus he was so exhausted himself that we agreed it was better to have one fully broken and one half-broken parent rather than two fully broken parents.

For the first time since going off to college, I became homesick for my mom and my sisters. I fantasized about them living around the corner, about swapping babies so that we could each squeeze in some personal time, about play dates with cousins, and support, you know, in the event that I had a nervous breakdown. I began to feel awkward in Eric's hometown. Like I was the First Lady of Sleep Deprivationstan, a country in the midst of a massive coup d'etat. Sitting on the sidelines with nothing of her own, per se. Since I was barely working, I had nothing to cling to for self-identity or purpose but babies, and there was enough clinging there already. Plus I knew I needed help, lots of it, and I was far more comfortable asking my own family for it than my in-laws.

Ruta Nonacs, MD, PhD, explains in *A Deeper Shade of Blue* that one of the most challenging aspects of caring for a young child in our culture is social isolation. "In traditional cultures, a woman's family gathers around the mother after the birth of a child," she writes. "They help her learn how to care for her child, [and they] provide companionship." Today most women are left to care for their baby alone.

My neighbors graciously offered to watch David for an hour and a half every Tuesday afternoon so that I could go swim. And on the weeks that my mother-in-law was around, sometimes she would take him for an hour, as well, so that I could get in another swim. While I realize that was two and a half hours more than most new moms got, it was hardly enough to sustain the rigorous mental-health program that I had worked prior to having babies: lots of sleep, exercise, meditation, spiritual reading, companionship, and therapy.

I was so lonely the year David was born that by the time he was nine months old, I formed a support group of mothers known as a play group. I distributed fliers on all the doors where I could see a stroller inside. I posted notices at businesses, delis, and coffee shops. Within a few weeks, twelve moms would show up at my door at 10 a.m. on Wednesday mornings. My neighbor, a single man in his fifties, wanted to be included after he saw out of his window all the attractive moms pouring into our house. I told him that he had to have had either an episiotomy or a C-section to join. So he stuck to fantasy baseball.

Support in those first months goes a long way toward preventing severe mental illness in new mothers, as well as treating the moms that already have one. One of my Beyond Blue readers recently told me that in some countries, like India, the treatment of choice is making sure people with severe mental illnesses, like schizophrenia, are living with and constantly accompanied by family members. And the results are sometimes no worse than those who are treated with medication in the United States.

During the worst of my depression, Eric and I decided to cash out a sizable amount of retirement funds so that we could hire the babysitting help that we needed in order for me to get well. I agreed to this only when two psychiatric nurses sat us down for a family meeting after three groups of patients who had started before me were discharged, and I sat in the same damn chair crying my eyes out.

"Therese is not going to get better as long as she has all of her caretaking responsibilities of young children," the nurses explained. So we bought our help at twelve bucks an hour, and it was the smartest investment we ever made.

I always feel like a whiner with a low threshold for pain when I candidly recount my early years of motherhood. But after I confided in my therapist about how little satisfaction I get from the job of motherhood—*not* to be confused with being a mother—on a daily basis, she grabbed from her bookcase a copy of *When Anger Hurts* by Matthew McKay, Judith McKay, and Peter Rogers. The authors summarize a few surveys that paint the real, not-so-Monet picture of parenthood and emotions, especially for those of us who are highly sensitive: less tolerant of loud noises, chaos, and just about everything else that kids create. In one survey, 41 percent of the parents rated their experience as "negative and frustrating."

While I was shocked to hear about those high numbers, I couldn't help but be relieved to know I wasn't alone, and that maybe the massive and annoying maternal grin I see gracing every cover of every tabloid in the grocery store when I'm checking out is lots and lots of Photoshop. And that maybe I'm not so much more delicate than all the other moms—perhaps I'm just more honest.

My Inner Child Has Escaped

"Making the decision to have a child—it's momentous," wrote Elizabeth Stone. "It is to decide forever to have your heart go walking around outside your body." Umm. This isn't a good thing if you have a bleeding heart, which I've discovered I have. You want to keep that bad boy tucked inside, where no one can see him. At least until dinner is over.

Seeing my little David quiver, jerk, and shudder with anxiety the way he did not only resurfaced my own childhood anxiety but also made me feel horribly responsible for his. It was one thing for me to be held captive by the biochemical, obsessive-compulsive mess in my brain, but quite another to helplessly watch my boy fight the waves of fear and panic for himself.

I agonized at seeing him engage in my war.

When David was two I took him to see a behavioral specialist because I knew his tantrums weren't normal.

"Describe them," the doctor said.

"For well over an hour he will scream, writhe and thrash his entire body, yelling with so much intensity that I check to see if he has broken a bone," I explained. "A few times, I paged his pediatrician because I feared that he swallowed a coin or something else on the floor and was experiencing bowel obstruction. The books I have read suggest that I do my best to ignore it. But I'm worried he's going to get a concussion the way he pounds his head against the wall or the kitchen tile floor."

"If he is banging his head that hard, then the best thing to do is to hold him tightly until he calms down," she said.

A few days later, during his next anxiety attack, I went to hold my son. He tried to squirm out of my arms, thrashing and writhing, but I held each of his limbs tightly so he couldn't escape. Controlling the wild thirty pounds was more difficult than swimming twenty-five meters in a pool with a panicked football player under my right arm, part of the test I passed to get my lifeguard license back in high school.

As I hugged him, tucking his little hands into mine, I felt the rush of panic back when I sat in my mom's lap all sweaty, panting after my bad dream about the ball of yarn that transformed into a bloodthirsty octopus about to strangle me and eat me for dinner.

As one scared kid trying to comfort another, I rocked David in my arms. I cried with him.

"It's okay," I said through my tears, trying to calm him and control his flailing limbs. "Breathe in," I whispered. "Breathe out."

God, did I want to absorb his anxiety—to throw it into my own collection of issues, to feel the terror for him so he wouldn't have to.

Instead, David absorbed mine.

Different studies have documented how depression in a new mother clearly affects her interactions with her baby or toddler. Depressed mothers are more withdrawn, less responsive to their infant's signals. "Their facial expressions and displays of emotion [are] more muted or flat, and their voices [are] monotone," explains Nonacs in *A Deeper Shade of Blue*. "They [remain] disengaged and [do] little to support their child's activities or exploration of the environment."

All that was true with me, even though I tried like hell to do everything that I thought good moms do: schedule play dates, check out kids' yoga, sign up for gymnastics, karate, and soccer.

Even worse, I couldn't stop crying. As much as I wanted to hide my tears from David, I was unable to control my sobbing. I bawled at the park, at church, at the grocery, at most of his play dates, parties, and activities. Between his third and fifth birthday I cried so much in front of him that I felt conflicted about reprimanding him for whining and tantrums. In his eyes, that was all I did.

I remember sitting on my son's bed one afternoon right before I was hospitalized. He was playing with his toy police car, guiding the car down the seams of the bedspread as if they were roads.

"You're in the back," he said.

"Why am I in the back?"

"Because you're bad."

"Why am I bad?"

"Because you cry so much."

"But . . ."

But what? How can you possibly explain severe clinical depression to a four-year-old boy who wants a stable, cheery mom—one that can take him to the park without breaking into tears behind a tree, or miss his great karate achievement because she had to bolt to the restroom and let her body shake with anxiety like a woman with severe Parkinson's.

I understand why people who haven't experienced severe depression believe that a mother who commits suicide is extremely selfish and totally careless in leaving her children to deal with that ugly and permanent baggage. But the truth is that I envisioned my suicide as an act of love for them. I was sure that by removing myself from the picture, I was affording David and Katherine a chance to lead a normal life, as they would be no longer victims to my moodiness and despair. The way I saw it, if Eric remarried a nice woman, my kids would be far better off than if I stuck around. So I began to search for a suitable bride and mother. I felt pressured to execute the plan as soon as possible, before David and Katherine formed memories, before my depression shattered their innocent lives.

I tear up whenever I write this, but it was *because of*, not despite of, my ferocious love for my children that I wanted to disappear.

How I wish I could take back that time—the two suicidal years between David's third and fifth birthday—and replace it with nothing but happy memories of my son and me at the park playing, shooting basketballs, coloring Spider-Man coloring books, filling the driveway with colored-chalk drawings.

But I can't go back. I can only move forward and work at this sanity thing as best I can with all the tools provided to me.

I have to stay well.

For myself.

For Eric.
For Katherine.
But especially for little David.

Armageddon in My Brain!

To explain the biochemical, neurological, and hormonal factors that triggered an Armegeddon inside my brain, I'd need a few neuroscientists, some high-definition brain imaging scans, and, of course, a crystal ball—because even in hindsight, I still don't totally understand *what* happened (low levels of mood-regulating neurotransmitters? shrinking hippocampus?) *where* (prefrontal cortex? amygdala?), and *why* (sleep deprivation? overproduction of cortisol?).

I do know that in the months after a woman gives birth she is more vulnerable than any other time for developing a severe mental illness, not just postpartum depression. Many specialists in the field of women's mental health believe this predisposition is because of the psychological stressors of this time coupled with the hormonal changes that occur in a woman's body.

In December 2006 Danish researchers published a fascinating study in the *Journal of the American Medical Association* that was the largest ever to look at postpartum depression and the first to consider other kinds of mental illness as different facets of serious postpartum depression.

The Danish study collected records from over a million first-time parents over a span of three decades, and found that the first three months after women have their first baby is riskiest, especially the first few weeks. During the first ten to nineteen days, new mothers were seven times more likely to be hospitalized with some form of mental illness than women with older infants. Compared to women with no children, new mothers were four times more likely to be hospitalized with mental problems.

In addition to the psychological stressors, sleep deprivation, power failure in the prefrontal cortex of my brain, and hormonal hysteria or confusion, I had the added benefit of developing a benign brain tumor—a growth in my pituitary gland.

What came first? My postpartum depression or the pituitary growth? I don't know. But this is what Mark S. Gold, MD, says about the pituitary gland in his book *The Good News About Depression* (I'm not crazy about that title):

> With all the hormones flowing to and through this gland, and its direct involvement with the hypothalamus and limbic system, anything that goes wrong with the pituitary is bound to affect mental life. Accordingly, since most of the body's hormones seem to be controlled by the same neurotransmitters that we believe are involved in mood disorders, the functioning of the pituitary and its client glands may well provide a window into the brains of depressed people. Many of our neuroendocrine tests for depression do indeed measure fluctuations in pituitary hormone output. Recently, magnetic resonance imaging (MRI) has been used to show active disease in the brain of depressed patients. MRIs clearly show that enlargement of the pituitary gland due to hypersecretion can provoke depression and vice versa.

Granted, given my childhood anxiety, adolescent eating disorder, high-school substance abuse, and college depression, I was pretty much hanging out in the waiting room of the Severe Mental Illness Club in the years after I graduated from Saint Mary's

College, wearing those "Life is good" T-shirts with a guy fishing, playing golf, or sleeping in a hammock.

But when my babies were born, I was invited inside and up-graded to a platinum-level membership: exclusive to those of us who may never graduate from talk therapy, require regular check-ins with doctors specializing in mental health (*psychiatrists*), and, in general, expend ten or twenty times the amount of effort on our mental-health programs as "normal" folks. Yeah! I'm in!

And with just four simple steps!

30 Ways Motherhood Is Like Mental Illness

Tracy Thompson begins her thoughtful book *The Ghost in the House: Motherhood, Raising Children, and Struggling with Depression* with two brilliant sentences: "Motherhood and depression are two countries with a long common border. The terrain is chilly and inhospitable, and when mothers speak of it at all, it is usually in guarded terms, or in euphemisms."

I can think of a few other—actually, thirty—ways motherhood is like a mental illness:

1. Five years into both of them, plastic surgery is your only way of looking young again.
2. There's only one boss, and it's best if that's you.
3. In both, you have to handle a lot of crap.
4. Both require deep breathing.
5. Time-outs are encouraged—especially for Mom. Psych-ward stays count for this.
6. Both feel like you're being pecked to death by a bird.
7. You must learn on the spot—pop quizzes are thrown at you every half hour.
8. Both drive you insane, of course.
9. Both are full of surprises and force you to tear up any script you may have written for your life.

10. They require a support system, discipline, and a ton of self-control.
11. You have to get out of bed in the morning for both.
12. Bedtime often spells relief.
13. Both take a chunk from your heart but give it back to your soul.
14. You never graduate from or complete your responsibilities.
15. You get used to frozen dinners, canned soup, and spats with your spouse.
16. You must sort out tons of advice, much of it horribly shallow and not at all useful.
17. Both benefit from lots of sunshine and time at the park.
18. They are tolerated best with a sense of humor.
19. Both can make you fat if you're not careful.
20. They are more challenging to the soul than the Spiritual Exercises of St. Ignatius.
21. A bad day of either is more physically exhausting than an Olympic-distance triathlon.
22. After only a few years they transform you into a more compassionate and loving human being, possibly a candidate for a Nobel Peace Prize.
23. With them comes a lot of wisdom and patience, possibly world peace.
24. A love for your kid(s) keeps you going through both.
25. You have to strike that difficult balance between keeping busy but not too busy.
26. The mornings and evenings are typically the hardest.
27. Stress complicates things. Best to avoid it as much as possible.
28. Comparing yourself to others will paralyze you.
29. There's no going back.
30. Your best is all you have, and that's good enough.

Chapter Six

"Honey, I Think It's Time!"

The Day I Cracked

I wish psychiatrists sent depressives home with instructions on when to go to the hospital similar to the ones obstetricians give to pregnant women once they reach 37 weeks of gestation: when your contractions last for a minute each and are five minutes apart, start the ignition!

According to J. Raymond DePaulo, Jr., MD, professor of psychiatry and director of the Affective Disorders Clinic at the Johns Hopkins University School of Medicine:

> The need for hospitalization arises if a person is endangered because he or she is suicidal, or so paranoid or so irritable that he or she is threatening or exhibiting violent behavior. Similarly urgent measures are called for if the ill person has developed hallucinations or delusions or is so confused as to be unable to care for basic personal needs.

But that decision isn't usually made as neatly as that paragraph reads. Each psych-ward experience is different, and no two doctors judge the decision to enter one in the same way. There's a whole lot of guesswork involved—which is frightening, really, because severely depressed people often cannot process all the information that needs to be considered before reserving a room at the hospital or psychiatric facility.

"How did you know it was time to go to the hospital?" a friend asked me the other day, deliberating on whether or not to go herself.

"I didn't," I replied. "My friends did."

In hindsight, I wonder why my therapist didn't urge me to commit myself months before I did. I talked about wanting to die most of my hour with her. Because it was all I thought about. That idea, and no other, gave me relief. But I guess since I had been depressed for so long and hadn't attempted suicide before, she felt I wasn't a threat to myself.

Eric didn't recognize my dangerous state, either. He was used to seeing me with a Kleenex in my hand, because I cried during 80 percent of my waking hours. Seriously: I sobbed while I ate, cooked, peed, showered, ran, cleaned, and fornicated. And that went on for a few twenty-four-hour periods, like at least 150.

Friends and family knew I was sick, so they told me to do things that worked for them: yoga, meditation, prayer, fish-oil capsules, massage, and lots of mind control. They tried to help me with the tools that were in their closets, but for something as complex and delicate as bipolar disorder, you absolutely need the right instruments.

Sometimes an outsider has the sharpest vision, like an out-of-town sister amazed by how much your kids have grown since she saw them last.

It was two girlfriends who hadn't seen me all summer who convinced me to pack my bags.

When David's preschool started back up for the year in September 2005, I joined my friend Christine for dinner after David's and her boys' karate class. When she arrived home she called another friend, Joani.

"I'm worried sick about Therese," she said. "She sat at the table like a zombie, not able to follow the conversation. She's lost a ton of weight. She was crying at karate. . . . The last person I saw that depressed is dead. We've got to do something."

The next day Joani knocked on the door. I was in my robe because I was trying out the advice of some stupid magazine article: if you surprise your partner with sexy lingerie at lunch you won't feel depressed. You see, I was already doing all the basics—taking meds, exercising, going to therapy, meditating, journaling, working with a doctor—so I would experiment with any and all advice on how to get those dang neurotransmitters to text-message each other like they were supposed to (LOL, TMI, BFF), force the nerve endings to sprout like tulips in March, and widen the hippocampus a tad.

Eric had come home ten minutes earlier and said sex sounded great, but first he needed to eat something. So as he ate the chef salad I made for him, I poked at mine, and then heard Joani let herself in, as usual.

Confident in her three months of sobriety—after going away to some recovery ranch in Texas—she immediately launched into her diatribe about why I should get shipped off somewhere, too.

"Chrissy couldn't sleep last night, she was so worried about you after seeing you at karate and dinner," she said. "She told me the last person she saw that depressed is now dead."

She paused, and then started arguing her second line of reasoning.

"I've been a nurse for most of my adult life, Therese, and I know the signs. I know the symptoms. . . . You need to do something. Now."

"Like what?" I lashed back angrily. "I've only tried fourteen medication combinations. I see my doctor several times *a week!* I'm working out like Lance bloody Armstrong. I'm in therapy. I'm praying like a blessed mystic. I don't drink. I don't smoke. I take my vitamins and supplements. I have cut out caffeine and most sweets. I write down all my damn blessings, list everything for which I'm grateful in my journal every morning. I really don't know what else there is to do, Joani!"

I started to sob, voicing the frustration and helplessness that I had held inside most of the summer.

For my friend to hear.

For my husband to hear.

For me to hear.

"For God's sake, look at me! I'm forcing myself to buy and wear some stupid lingerie because some cheesy damn article said that it will get me to stop crying."

I waited a minute and then asked her this: "You're the nurse. Tell me. What the hell do I have to do to feel better?"

I wiped my nose with my white robe and I looked down at my untouched salad. Another bag of produce wasted.

"Maybe it's time you check yourself in," she answered.

"To an insane asylum?" I retorted. I conjured images in my mind of the stale place where I used to visit Mary Lou. I pictured my godmother teaching me how to light her cigarette, as she sat next to three women in paper robes staring into space, with absolutely nothing—not even a night-light—going on upstairs, like corpses that hadn't been buried yet. *Oh God, no. Not there. I can't go there*, I thought to myself. *I can't go there.*

"To the hospital," she answered.

"Dr. R. says that it's normal to crash after a hypomania like mine—that my brain is just adjusting to the meds. He told me that sometimes you get worse before you get better," I explained

"Not for three months, Therese. You shouldn't be getting worse steadily for three months. Something isn't right."

I looked at Eric.

He was wearing a blank stare, showing no expression or emotion.

I wondered what he was thinking as he sat there in the maple-wood chair he picked out when we first married. He seemed scared and tired. I noticed a few more gray hairs behind his ears and an extra wrinkle on his forehead. *I wonder if he would have married me nine years ago had he known I was crazy,* I thought.

Then he looked at me.

"Maybe it's time, Therese," he said. "Maybe it's time."

I rose from my chair and walked over to my desk. I prayed my simple mantra, the one I had been repeating for the last four months: "God, be with me." And then I picked up the phone and left a message with my doctor's assistant.

"Just tell him I went to the hospital," I told her.

Looking back, I know that it was absolutely the right thing to do.

A person can't fight suicidal urges forever. Eventually willpower wilts. And that day was getting closer for me. I couldn't continue to expend 99.9 percent of my energy on *not* killing myself, on not pursuing one of ten plans I had designed to end my life, since everything in me gravitated toward the curtain of death.

My friends knew that Eric was planning on taking the kids to California to visit their newborn cousin, Tia, for four days. They knew I shouldn't be left alone with my stash of prescriptions that could stop my pulse. These two fellow moms intuited or suspected that I might take my life while the family was in California, and they postulated from my empty gaze that I was too doped up on sedatives and antipsychotics to hear the rational voice argue against suicide without anyone around.

They were right.

My psychiatrist at that time, whom I now refer to as Pharmaceutical King, Pharma King for short, had tried fourteen different medications in three months. And I'm not talking aspirin. He pulled out the heavy-duty atypical neuroleptics or antipsychotics: Zyprexa, Seroquel, Risperdal, and Geodon. When I worsened on the antipsychotics, he supplemented them with some anticonvulsants (Lamictal) and a new antiepileptic called Trileptal in case . . . I don't know . . . I had a seizure?

I took these longer-than-four-syllables drugs on top of almost every kind of SSRI: Celexa, Lexapro, Prozac, Paxil, and Zoloft. Plus he told me to not hesitate one iota about popping as many milligrams of Ativan that I needed. And to take some Valium at night.

By August 2005, I was nearly delusional and psychotic. I was taking something like 16 pills a day: consisting of 4 mg of Ativan, 10 mg of Valium, 300 mg of Trileptal, 60 mg of Cymbalta, 20 mg of Celexa, and 200 mg of Lamictal. My insides were toxic, and my body finally said, *No more.*

I should have clued in to the fact that I almost always shared the waiting room of Pharma King's office with a pharmaceutical rep, and that many of them had frequented the place so often and knew the receptionist so well that the two would catch up on gossip: "Yep, I started my community college classes last night, and so far so good, thanks for asking." I should have raised an eyebrow at his closets stocked with every new drug on the market; they were crammed with as many pharmaceuticals as my dad's closets used to be with bottles of vodka and rum. I should have inquired why he was so down on older, better-researched drugs like Lithium.

I should have been smarter than to trust Pharma King. Yet every reliable source, including both my primary-care physician and my therapist, confirmed that he was the best psychiatrist in Annapolis.

He's the professional. I have to trust him. He knows better than ME, I periodically reminded myself.

I was too sick to trust my own instincts, too insecure to make my own judgment, too deafened by all those damn pills to hear my rational voice. Like so many mentally ill patients, I lacked the confidence to acknowledge that I could be in the hands of a very dangerous man.

But the professionals at Laurel Regional Hospital, the closest hospital with a psych unit, recognized how overmedicated I was the afternoon Eric dragged me into the emergency room.

The nurse who evaluated me in the emergency room asked me all the questions I predicted:

"Do you have suicidal ideations?"

"Yes."

"Do you have any plans?"

"Yes." *Hello???? Does a golfer carry golf balls?? Here's one fact about me, lady: when I set my mind to something, I accomplish it. I'm not a wannabe, I'm a gonnabe . . . so there's no fantasizing about suicide without ten very detailed plans and twenty more if those fail.*

Eric looked at me, horrified. It was the first time he heard me say out loud that I was actively planning my death, and it was only a matter of time before I was going to execute it.

The nurse didn't flinch. "Let's take you upstairs and get you some help. But first, how do you spell your name?"

"Like Theresa without the *a* at the end," I answered. "There were too many Theresas in my fourth-grade class, and I wanted to be more like my patron saint, St. Therese of Lisieux."

"Interesting," she replied. "My middle name is Theresa, too. I was also named after the Little Flower."

I got chills. And I knew I was going to be okay.

So I hugged Eric good-bye. I kissed him, and then the nurse, Monica Theresa, walked me upstairs to the psych unit.

The first patient I met was a psychotic woman in her fifties pushing an IV rack, dressed in a paper hospital robe with her polyester striped underwear hanging out the back, yelling "Cocaine! Cocaine!" up and down the halls of the unit. And I thought to myself, *There goes any warm fuzzy I had about St. Therese leading this stage of my recovery. What in the hell did I just do? Eric, save me! Damn it! They have my cell phone. I'm stuck here. With crazies! For at least four days!*

I unpacked my things in my room, imagining that I was at a Trappist retreat, that I was merely trying to mature my soul a tad so that I had a better shot at peace and sanity. And then I was asked to check in with the doctor.

Dr. T was a kind man whose calm disposition helped assuage the panic induced by the psychotic woman with the granny underwear yelling "Cocaine!" down the halls.

He looked at my list of prescriptions and blurted out: "Why did your doctor put you on all this crap?"

"That's a good question," I responded.

He shook his head.

Sitting in his office, I knew then and there that God was with me, and that this was right and good. I knew that even as Laurel Hospital's psych ward was no Ritz Carlton with complimentary massages and room service, it was still a safe place for my body to detox from all the atypical antipsychotics, antiepileptics, and benzodiazepines swimming around in my bloodstream, from the life-threatening drug experiment I was part of. Dr. T and nurse Monica Theresa, without realizing it, furnished me with the ultimate weapon that I could use in my fight against depression: *hope*. And Laurel Hospital gave me what I needed desperately but hadn't had the confidence to pursue: a second opinion.

Dr. T began to wean me off all the newer drugs—especially the atypical antipsychotics I couldn't tolerate and the dangerous amount of benzodiazepines—while starting Lithium, a less sexy but more reliable mood stabilizer; Wellbutrin (a dopamine reuptake inhibitor that has less sexual side effects than the SSRIs, not that I was going to orgasm before a new US president was elected); and two small doses of Klonopin, instead of the handful of Ativan I had been popping throughout the day.

He came by my room an hour or so after my initial evaluation. I was looking out the window, fantasizing about running around the Naval Academy. It was a crisp September day, not a cloud in the sky, and I wanted so badly to feel the sun on my shoulders, to let the monarch butterflies land on me as I cooled off and stretched after my run. I wanted to be part of the world, not separate from it. The glass pane on which I leaned my forehead felt like the bars of a prison cell: protecting the world from me, not the other way around. Even as I shuddered at life, I yearned to be in it—not a in nuthouse with only two community phones and absolutely no privacy. I wondered what I could possibly gain by being locked up here. *Can't they just send me home with the new meds?*

Dr. T knocked on the door. When I looked up, he read my facial expressions like a medical chart. He stepped inside my room and handed me some literature on bipolar disorder.

"Look," he said. "I know you think you have nothing in common with these people."

Now, Doctor, I thought to myself, *what makes you say that? My room-mate's wrists are wrapped in gauze from her slashing them. I mean, jeez, at least I picked a dozen classier ways to go. Slashing wrists? That's so white trash.*

"Try to view your time here as a seminar," he said. "Learn everything you can about bipolar disorder and try to get some rest. Both will aid your recovery. And don't worry about everyone else. You are here for you."

I returned to the community room where everyone was gathered around the TV watching reporters interview people in New Orleans who had lost their families, homes, jobs, churches—their everything—to Hurricane Katrina less than two weeks before. Their pain was palpable, and I felt incredibly guilty for being depressed, for occupying a hospital bed when these poor people didn't have a place to stay.

They have a reason to cry, I told myself. *You're just a damn wimp.*

I ambled back to my room, sat on my bed, and cried. Then I composed this letter to myself, but I think someone else held the pen:

> *Dear Therese,*
>
> *Go inside. Deep inside.*
>
> *And find the girl, the woman, the person you truly are.*
>
> *Now embrace her. Throw your arms around her.*
>
> *Kiss her. Love her.*
>
> *You are battling a horrific disease. Even though people are dying in Katrina's wake, you are waging your own intimidating battle.*
>
> *It is real. It is not imaginary.*
>
> *But you must find the love, the faith, within yourself to go face to face with this monster. The healing energy must come from you.*
>
> *You must find those reserves inside, hiding in the pockets of pain created over the years, pockets of fear of not being good enough or strong enough or smart enough, the fear of finding yourself and being yourself and liking yourself.*
>
> *You must go deep inside and love yourself, not for what you have done or how you appear from the outside, but for who you are.*
>
> *There is where your healing is.*

I did what the kind doctor told me to do: I learned everything I could about bipolar disorder, borrowing literature and watching videos in my free time between group therapy sessions. During this time, I inched a bit closer toward accepting the diagnosis of manic depression. But I was far from wrapping my arms around it because I still couldn't get past the picture of Mary Lou, dead, in the garage. *That's bipolar.* If I admitted I was bipolar and labeled myself as such, therein lies my future, I thought.

I could clearly recognize my symptoms of depression: overwhelming feelings of sadness and grief; apathy, or loss of interest and pleasure in activities once enjoyed; sleep problems; decreased energy or fatigue; noticeable changes in appetite and weight; an inability to concentrate or think; indecisiveness; and recurrent thoughts of death and suicide. In fact, underneath the words *Major Depression* in the *DSM-IV* is written: "Read Therese's diary."

But I still had trouble recognizing the mania, or even *hypomania*, since I was diagnosed with bipolar II—the "softer," nonpsychotic variety, the Diet Coke of bipolar, as Dr. Evil would say in *Austin Powers*.

And yet, the signs were all there:

- inflated self-esteem or grandiosity ("No, really. I *am* going to pen the next *The Devil Wears Thongs*, followed by *A Thousand Splendid Naps*, *The Blimp Runner*, and *Who Moved My Keys?*");
- decreased need for sleep ("Eric, I'm telling you, midnight is the best time to e-mail colleagues; the words flow better the second half of the night.")
- more energy (*That 100 laps went by quickly! I think I'll swim another set.*);
- more talkative than usual and talking very quickly ("Hello, stranger! Did you know DavidknowshowtotiehisshoesandIate fourKitKatstoday?");
- racing thoughts or a rush of ideas (*I know! A new line of greeting cards to comfort those whose alter personalities aren't getting along and whose inner children are missing, for families scheduling an intervention a week before the holidays, and for unstable folks with mean employers, incarcerated siblings, and bad therapists; a new reality show called* The Playgroup, *where you vote an annoying mom and her kid off every week; a Web site called LoveGenies.com, the best love advice on the web!*);
- distractibility ("Don't call me on my cell phone because I

don't know where it is. Where did I put my keys? My car? My kids?");
- increase in goal-directed activity ("Why do you say that it's overkill to attempt to write three books, build a Web site, cohost a radio show, and organize a school fund-raiser this year while taking care of two preschoolers?");
- bizarre thought patterns or loose cognitive connections (*SpongeBob ate two Krabby Patties at the Krusty Krab today, therefore God is telling me to adopt two orphaned children from Kuwait.*);
- excessive involvement in pleasurable activities that have a high potential for painful consequences (Ummm. Can't think of any of those!).

Nowhere in the *DSM-IV* did it say "experiences a propensity to tell inappropriate jokes—'What's the worst thing about being an atheist? No one to talk to during sex!'—to colleagues in suits," or "sends dozens of e-mails to coworkers at midnight AND USES ALL CAPS JUST TO MAKE SURE THEY ARE PAYING ATTENTION," or "jots down on a pad of paper—that she keeps in her pocket as well as one in each room of the house because she can never be too prepared—so many ideas that she's convinced are brilliant! brilliant! brilliant! And she has to record them before they fly away. So she scribbles away as she walks downtown to get more coffee BECAUSE SHE WANTS THIS FEELING TO LAST AND YOU CAN NEVER DRINK TOO MUCH COFFEE." Not once did the shrink manual mention any of those.

So I wasn't bipolar! Thank you very much!

Upon my discharge from the hospital five days later, the doctors and nurses recommended that I participate in an outpatient program, which included the same intense group therapy and sessions with a psychiatrist—a colleague of Dr. T—I'd received at the hospital. That way I could continue treatment without having to sleep there and wake up to a nurse taking my vitals. I got to skip breakfast in the community room, as well. The partial-hospitalization plan, as the nurses referred to it, was only supposed to last two weeks. But for the next two months, I drove the fifty minutes to Laurel Hospital four times a week.

On the way there, I'd listen to meditation tapes, on the way back spiritual affirmations. I would come home and run six miles, during which I prayed prayed prayed and imagined myself as a serene and calm woman, in a pink silk dress with my hair up in a clip, holding a rose, symbolizing health. In our group, we practiced such visualization techniques.

In group therapy, I divulged to fellow patients everything that was on my mind. *Everything.* I had never been so candid with a group of strangers. Because, for the first time in my life, I didn't care if they liked me or not. I was there to get well, and I would do whatever it took.

One day I discussed all of my suicidal plans. I brought in a plastic bag holding all my prescriptions from Pharma King—about thirty bottles of drugs—that I'd been keeping in case I got desperate again, in case I wanted to take my life.

I threw the bag in the center of our circle.

"Here," I said to the nurse running the group. "Take them. I am no longer considering this option."

I continued to see my therapist twice a week. I began to attend 12-step support groups again. I started going to church with more regularity. I meditated every day.

I don't know, to this day, what else I could have done to feel better.

I still wanted to die.

I watched three separate groups of patients come into the

partial-hospitalization program as anxious and depressed as I was and then, after two weeks of group therapy and psychiatric evaluations, gain enough composure to be honorably discharged. I, on the other hand, was finally let go from the program simply because my insurance would no longer pay for treatment.

I didn't blame them for saying I needed more therapy and supervision. Angry and despondent, I hadn't exactly been an ideal patient. One morning in group therapy, I had slammed down my writing journal and my copy of *What Happy People Know*.

"What does it take? What the hell does it take to feel better?" I yelled. "Why are you guys getting better and I'm not?" I brought my hands to my face and started to bawl. I felt completely frustrated, tired of trying every cognitive-behavioral technique I knew, practicing relaxation methods, exercising regularly, eating well, composing gratitude lists, and praying with Scripture every morning.

Nothing seemed to work.

On my last day in the program I bid farewell to the nurses and asked for my bag of pills back.

"We can't do that, Therese," one said. "Why do you want it back?"

"Because . . . I'm seeing a new doctor now, trying to get my meds straight. And she will probably try some of the medications I was on before. I don't want to spend the extra money filling the prescriptions."

That was neither the truth nor a lie. It qualified as a Clintonism.

"We'll have to phone Eric first and make sure he knows that you have the bag and that he'll have to keep it in a safe place."

"Sure. Make the call," I said.

Five minutes later, the nurse handed me my bag.

I felt like my seventeen-year-old self again with a stash of vodka.

It would be so easy, I told myself. *To make this all go away. To make this go away for good.*

I walked out to the car thinking about what one of the nurses told me just a few days before: that the outpatient program helps 95 percent of patients. Wondering where I had gone wrong, I ripped off my hospital badge and climbed into my car.

I wept the whole way home.

I also issued God an ultimatum:

I can't do it anymore, God. I'm done. I can't go on feeling this way. I've been doing my part. I'm working with a doctor. I'm retraining my thoughts. I'm exercising. I'm trying to be grateful. I'm praying. But listen, it's not working, and unless you give me a sign that I'm supposed to hang on, I'm out of here. God damn it! I am so out of here! Give me a blessed sign! Or else I am out of here!

I looked over at the bag of prescriptions. I had two hours until the kids got home, four hours until I'd have to hand this bag over to Eric.

It's now or never, I thought. *Here's your chance. For silence. For peace. For a new beginning for the kids. For Eric.*

I was bent over the steering wheel practically hyperventilating, I was crying so hard. I just stayed there repeating the words: *God be with me. God be with me. God be with me.*

I climbed out of the car, holding the bag. My shoulders slumped over, I used my last reserve of energy to pick up the mail from the box outside my house. Shuffling through the envelopes, I saw a letter from a woman named Rose, whom I had met in Buffalo almost a year before, when I had given a speech to an audience of over five hundred Catholics. I told them the story of St. Theresa's novenas in my life and the presence of roses in times of trial.

I ripped open the envelope to find a card with an image of St. Therese surrounded by roses and the words "I will spend my heaven in doing good upon earth." Inside the card I found my name and an announcement that a novena would be offered for my intention by Carmelite nuns, St. Therese's order, as requested by Rose.

My eyes were already swollen with tears when I saw the medal of St. Therese that Rose had enclosed. It was an exact copy of the one I had been carrying in my pocket ever since the day my depression set in. On the front of the medal was a profile of St. Therese; on the back, above a crucifix and bouquet of roses, was the inscription "After my death I will let fall a shower of roses."

And I'm here to tell that story.

How I Met My Guardian Angel

Sometimes, if you are lucky and brave, you can watch someone who's met with serious illness or loss and do the kind of restoration that I suspect we are here on earth to do," writes Anne Lamott in *Plan B*.

That person in my life is my guardian angel, Ann.

Navigating blindly through the sharp twists and steep climbs of my manic depression has been the most terrifying task of my life so far. It would have been twice as harrowing had I not been guided by a woman whom I believe God sent to me for direction, companionship, comfort, and consolation.

I met Ann on a train from New York City to Baltimore, a train neither of us were supposed to be on. This was before I started working with Pharma King, back when I was under the care of the first psychiatrist in the series of seven. It had been only two weeks since she had suggested that I had bipolar disorder and should start taking a mood stabilizer.

Because of an Amtrak strike, there were few trains leaving the city. I snuck on an earlier one to guarantee I'd get home that night.

With people standing in the bathroom, in the café car, and in the aisles, I searched for some open space. A woman in her fifties, with platinum hair and a gentle face, moved her bags from the seat next to her and said to me, "You can sit here."

As I sank into the seat, I thought about my manic day: throwing twenty-five book ideas at my agent, telling inappropriate jokes to a colleague—"What's the difference between a golf ball and a G spot? A man will look twenty minutes for his golf ball!"—and scribbling furious notes about random thoughts in between my meetings.

Suddenly, a gorgeous woman seated in front of me got up to leave. She didn't look a day older than twenty-five, so when I heard her mention her adult children living in New York, I said to my train partner, "Genes. Some people get all the good ones."

"Ha," she replied. "And I got mental illness."

"Me too," I said.

"I'm manic depressive," she said.

"Me too," I responded.

We spent the entire three hours taking about diagnoses, medications, psychiatrists, and therapists. Ann told me about the suicide of her father when she was seven. I told her that although I had been recently diagnosed as bipolar, I didn't like the idea of taking a mood stabilizer.

I was in a fair amount of denial at the time. Because I was so very scared of becoming Mary Lou.

Ann jabbered on about all the politicians and celebrities who suffer from our illness and wrote down the titles of books, such as *An Unquiet Mind* by Kay Redfield Jamison, that could better inform me. She was articulate, funny, and seemed halfway normal!

Although I had manically transcribed our entire dialog I forgot to get her number. But in my rush to get off the train, I left my cell phone on my seat. When I realized I had lost it, I used our home phone to dial its number. My angel answered, and she gave me her phone number.

I carried Ann's number in my pocket everywhere I went, especially after I descended into the worst of my depression, a few weeks after meeting her. Sometimes I phoned her daily to hear a nugget of wisdom. "It won't always be like this," she said, and I believed her because, unlike other friends, she had been there. A woman of strength and determination, she stuck her tongue out at her diagnosis and went on living her life.

Recently I came across an e-mail Ann sent me after I'd shared some of my writing with her. Ann wrote:

Dear Therese,

Our train ride, conversations, and knowing you needed an optimistic person in your life, is something I will never forget. You were so vulnerable and frightened, using laughter and comedy when you might have been better off crying. It was a frightening time for you, and I was always glad to be there for you with practical, honest, and medically correct suggestions. You were getting a lot of misguided advice, were surrounded by people who don't know the pain, panic, and suicidal thoughts of one whose brain is out of control and giving the wrong messages.

Once one walks in the door of a good psychiatrist [and I repeat GOOD psychiatrist], the scientist, and finds a good therapist as well as cognitive-thinking help, she realizes how alone she has been most of her life.

Your success is shown in your writing, activities, and care for your family. They have to be thanking God that you are back. You were always there, and the bad chemicals have nothing to do with your talents, inner beauty, and writing. You are on your way, and the time is right.

You are too good to me. I simply tell you what has happened in my life.

Love,

Ann

Ann articulates a very important message that I think all depressives should be reminded of when stuck in the Black Hole: that the person underneath the illness never goes away; she only waits for proper treatment in order to surface again.

Chapter Seven

Mind over Spoon

When Yoga and Meditation Aren't Enough

Despite the fact that I knew Ann was right about working with the right doctor, when I left the hospital outpatient program, my faith in traditional medicine tiptoed out the door with me. I resented Pharma King for nearly killing me with all his antipsychotic cocktails—and all the nurses at Laurel Hospital who quickly came to his defense whenever I complained about his overmedicating.

"Are you sure you gave him an accurate medical history?" they asked me while I was in the outpatient program. "Did you describe the same symptoms you've described in our groups?"

No, I thought to myself, I fabricated a whole other set of symptoms for him so that I could try out the fancy new antipsychotics he mentioned. They sounded so appealing with their side effects of thirty extra pounds, dry mouth, and dizziness, and I really liked their names. Plus, how comforting to know that should I ever start to seizure, I was on the right drug! WHAT THE HELL KIND OF QUESTION IS THAT???

Throughout my outpatient group therapy program, I grew increasingly uncomfortable with the immediate jump from a patient's expression of frustration or confusion to the nurses' suggestion that they up the prescriptions of Seroquel, Risperdal, or Geodon. *For God's sake, let her work through her negative thoughts with the group. Maybe she can learn a helpful technique from us, or some insight that would help her. Do we always have to increase the drugs?* I thought to myself several times. The teacher's pet—"We're so proud of you! You've made incredible progress!!!"—was a woman who walked and talked like Franken-stein because she was on so many meds. I was tempted to knock on her head several mornings: *Hello?????? Anyone in there?* She had zippo confidence in her own reasoning skills. After every sentence, she'd look to the nurses for their approval and for directions on what to say next.

"It's an industry," a fellow patient, Dan, said to me one day in between sessions. "Didn't you think it was slightly odd that no one from your inpatient group was transferred here but you?"

He paused. "It's because you could afford it. They thought you had insurance that would pay for it. Other patients don't. So they get pushed out the door after three days locked up in a psych ward."

The day that I brought in the bag of drugs from Pharma King, Dan said to the nurses: "I'm sorry, but prescribing that many drugs in such a short time span is criminal. That's a *Dr. Phil* show right there."

I agreed with him. But we were the black sheep in the group; we were the ones "getting in the way of our progress," as the nurses explained it, because we questioned everything they fed us. That's why, the nurses basically insinuated, we didn't thrive like the others.

But the others hadn't been poisoned like I had. They hadn't learned the hard way the most basic truth of Life Survival 101— that you never, ever relinquish your authority to someone not named "I" or "me" or "self." Drug me once, shame on you. Drug me twice, shame on me.

I eventually left the colleague of Dr. T because the whopping ten minutes she could afford her patients—because she accepted insurance—wasn't enough time to describe my very complex symptoms. I didn't like having to do so much of her job for her, like diagnose myself. *Dude, I'm not the one with an MD!*

Not that any of the doctors after her were better. One psychiatrist claimed that all I really had to do was to sleep more, that once I was rested, all would be peachy in my world. *Hello? Is that what you say to a person who has five detailed suicidal plans? "Try a nap?"* A shrink after that asked me if I liked myself, and when I responded, "Um, no, not at this particular time . . . thus the desire to kill myself," he diagnosed me with borderline personality. Apparently those guys don't get giddy when they gaze into the mirror.

Every doctor who had the pleasure of being interrogated by me post Pharma King was met with a familiar skepticism that, for the most part, they didn't appreciate. Most resented my questions and the fact that I was well informed about bipolar disorder, that I could argue the pros and cons of different treatment philosophies. And I refused to work with anyone who didn't support my quest for better understanding of mood disorders.

In these doctors' offices, I also studied the pharmaceutical reps and their briefcases. Were they happy when they left? Too many smiles were a bad sign. How tight were the reps with the receptionist? If they knew why she bailed on boyfriend number one and why boyfriend number two hadn't yet introduced her to his parents, we were in trouble.

After meeting with a half dozen psychiatrists, I felt like a drug rep myself. I'm sure I averaged more time in the waiting room. The only difference was that I wasn't compensated by the doc's signature. They actually cost me. A large sum, by the time I handed all of them to the kind pharmacist I know on a first-name basis at Rite Aid. When I reached medication-combination 21, I was so frustrated by the search for a good shrink and so tired of experimenting with more drugs than I had fingers and toes, that I flushed my diagnosis of bipolar disorder, as well as all of traditional medicine, down the toilet.

Done.

Finished.

I stopped looking for a cure from drug-dispensing doctors and turned to the world of alternative therapies.

This seemed like a natural course of action. Because most of the advice from a chorus of friends at the time concentrated on "natural" cures like fish oil, acupuncture, Chinese herbs, homeopathic remedies, craniosacral therapy, yoga, and everything else you associate with the word *holistic*. Annapolis is an affluent, artistic city, where about 75 percent of the population subscribes to a radical interpretation of the Law of Attraction, keeps a copy of Rhonda Byrnes's *The Secret* in their bathroom, and would be ecstatic if Oprah ran for US president.

Everywhere I turned or asked for feedback, the answer kept coming back: *alternative medicine*. I began to believe advice like:

"Fish oil is all you need to correct the imbalances in your brain."

"You're allergic to all those drugs the psychiatrists have been giving you. They're toxic."

"You need a natural remedy . . . some organic supplements."

"Antidepressants suppress your emotions; they prevent you from getting to the source of your distress."

"You're beating a dead horse with this search for the right psychiatrist."

All of these so-called holistic experts recounted stories of people who had unwittingly bequeathed their personalities to traditional psychiatrists and allowed medication to steal their souls. Moreover, they told me it was happening to me, as well, and I had better see the light before getting sucked into the dark, ominous vortex of psych drugs.

My God! I thought to myself. *What if I never tell a dirty joke again?*

One evening after I'd decided to try the holistic route, my friend Sue came over to perform Reiki, a laying-on-of-hands-energy-healing technique developed in Japan in the late 1700s.

She held her hands over my head for an hour or two. I cried the entire time.

"Look at me and tell me who you see," she instructed me.

I looked up. I thought I saw Mary, Jesus' mother. *Or had she just mentioned Mary, and I wanted to please her so I said Mary?*

"Who do you see now?" Sue asked.

I looked up.

"Jesus?" I asked.

I was confused. *Was my brain telling me who to see to please her, or was I really being healed?* This is why I don't think hypnosis works on people pleasers. *No really, what do you want me to say? What do you want me to see? Just let me know and I'll say it!*

"There are so many other things you can do to heal besides take medication," Sue said after she finished the Reiki.

I wanted so badly to trust her.

Because I felt like I couldn't trust anyone anymore.

"People in the eastern hemisphere commission physicians to keep them healthy. The doctors aren't paid primarily when people are sick, like the system is here," another friend, Liz, explained to me the night of the Reiki. "The medical community in the US— it's all a racket, driven by drug companies. These pharmaceuticals are a business. A huge one. And an extremely dangerous one."

I couldn't argue against that. Having been Pharma King's pet guinea pig, and scorned by the psych nurses at Laurel for using my brain, I had evidence to support her case.

It was easy to believe that most traditional psychiatrists feed their patients a bunch of bull in order to get paid by the drug companies— because we know the insurance companies aren't paying them anymore—and that all I needed to do was learn how to center myself and get to my core. Like so many other times in my life, I reverted back to zebra, black-and-white thinking: all twenty-one medications plus electroconvulsive therapy, or nothing but yoga and green tea.

So, because of a few defective doctors and a bad experience in a hospital outpatient program, I turned my back on the fifteen years of research I had done on the topic of depression and psych meds—everything that I had learned about mental illness at Saint Mary's College and after.

As I began to wean completely off my drugs, I was barely able to function.

One afternoon I tried to chaperone Katherine to her field trip at the pumpkin patch, and as all the preschool moms climbed onto the back of a truck for a hayride, I sat there shaking and weeping on a pile of hay, wondering if hay pieced together would be strong enough to strangle myself.

"Are you okay?" one of the moms asked me.

"Fall allergies," I explained.

One evening Eric's boss took all of his employees and their spouses out to eat at a nice steak joint that their firm had designed. I remember gazing at Eric from across the table, appreciating his charm, his skill as an architect, his humor, and his cute dimples.

When are you going to get out of his life and let him go on to meet someone who can be a true partner? a voice began to say. *He doesn't love you. How can he? You're unlovable. No one can love a person who can't master her thoughts, a pathetic person like you who only makes messes in this world. Free him. Let him go. Kill yourself.*

I teared up and immediately excused myself to go to the bathroom. I stayed there until I could manage my breathing and hide my tears.

I made a series of mistakes that could have been deadly.

One afternoon I flew by a school bus that had pulled over to the side of the road, despite the fact that the driver had extended the red stop sign to make sure his kids could cross the street safely. My mind was racing so fast that it was unable to process what was happening in the present moment. Like the mad mathematician John Nash in the movie *A Beautiful Mind*, I was immersed in a different world inside my head, whirling with messages that I was simultaneously trying to make sense of and record on a pad of paper.

I got busted.

Someone sent Eric a photo of my car flying past the school bus, in an envelope with no return address.

"What the hell was going on with you? Why couldn't you stop for a bunch of schoolkids?" Eric asked me.

I couldn't respond. I didn't know what to say. It wouldn't make sense. Not to a rational set of ears, anyway.

Strike one.

Then one rainy night, I drove the kids to Annapolis's Seafood Market. With my head somewhere else, I turned into what I thought was an entrance. My car hit a high curb, and then I backed out into traffic, with two lanes of cars coming straight at me.

People honked and yelled at me out their windows, "Lady, what the hell are you on?"

I panicked and managed to drive the car up onto a curb to wait for the traffic to slow down, to figure out how the hell I was going to get myself out of this mess.

David tattled on me to Eric.

Strike two.

Shortly after that, I was driving Katherine to David's class Halloween party when I started to have a panic attack. Despite my efforts to breathe deeply, my heart was pounding so fast that my hands couldn't properly clutch the wheel, and I lost control. I hit the curb, causing a flat tire. Stranded there, I called Eric to bail me out. He came, and managed not to yell at me.

Instead he said, "I don't think you should drive until we get on top of this, Therese. . . . Give me your keys."

Strike three. Game over.

I had weaned off of my meds until I was down to just 50 mg of Zoloft, which, to treat bipolar disorder, was like popping a few baby aspirin to remedy a war wound. I intended to get off of everything, to go cold turkey as I turned to the alternative-therapy world to heal me, to grant me my miracle.

I started with acupuncture.

Now I have to admit, I wasn't crazy about the idea of a short Chinese man forming a necklace of needles on my collarbone and other energy centers. But when I researched why acupuncture could help treat depression—that the needles can aid the flow of energy, or *chi*—I invited the little Chinese man into my world.

I was fascinated by brain studies indicating that acupuncture can serve as a natural painkiller. *You want a shot of vodka? Go see Dr. Chi!* And that even though it seems to the person wearing a needle necklace and bracelet that the Chinese guy has absolutely no idea what he is pricking, he is able to read your body like a map: by stimulating one acupuncture point on the little toe, he can trigger activity in the brain's visual cortex. If the right energy centers are targeted, acupuncture can generate the release of endorphins and other brain chemicals. At least according to the research that I read. Arthur Margolin of Yale University School of Medicine says that this Chinese tradition activates the parasympathetic part of the nervous system, which has a calming effect.

I was very open to it, and I had no agenda in wanting it to fail. But after six sessions, I still could not stop crying in the half hour that I was to remain still with the needles prickling my energy centers.

"When you get sad?" Dr. P asked me during my first visit.

"I've always suffered from depression," I explained.

"Uh?" he looked up. "Don't understand. Don't understand. I only have one day in my life I sad. Just one day. Don't understand."

Well, that's very nice, I thought to myself. *BUT I PRETTY MUCH WANT TO DIE ALL THE TIME! SO GET POKING!*

He would pop in on me fifteen minutes into our session and find me shaking and crying.

"Acupuncture don't work if you don't relax," he said. "You must relax. You must relax." He then turned on the meditation tape, which made me want to pee, not relax.

Super. I've failed at one more damn thing, I thought.

One day I was especially shaky. I was weaning off the last of the sedatives, and the detox was hell.

"When you walk in, I see black," he said.

I find you charming as well, I thought.

"You treat chronic problems like depression and anxiety with acupuncture and herbs," Dr. P said. "You treat acute illness, like cancer, with medication."

His logic made sense to me. *Because it's bad to be on any medication long-term. Everyone knows that.*

Yet I experienced no relief from the sessions, or from the expensive Chinese herbs I was taking. The only change in myself that I noticed was that my urine smelled like it does after I eat asparagus or get a massage.

Dr. P placed three magnets on my earlobes. "This one, *peace.* This, *joy.* This, *calm,*" he said. "You need press once an hour, okay? You feel better."

I don't know if Dr. P knows what obsessive-compulsive disorder is. If he did, I suspect he wouldn't have given me that assignment. *If I'm supposed to press once, than guess what—897 times is even better!!!! And holy crap! I lost one in the shower. Oh no, God, oh no! There goes joy! Bye, joy!*

I think Dr. P was ready for me to leave after the sixth session. So I gave the short Chinese man a nice hug and never went back.

Next I made an appointment with a naturopath. He gave me a homeopathic remedy that I was to shake, hold upright, and hit against a telephone book ten times. He told me to bang it "as hard as your fist hits the table if you lift your fist one foot above the table and let it drop by itself." I kept those instructions handy in case I ever wrote a book entitled *The Ten Best Ways to Waste Your Money.* Then I was supposed to squeeze six to seven drops of this solution—the components of which I hadn't a clue—into four ounces of distilled water, using a container made of glass, *not ceramic.* Next came stirring the solution for fifteen seconds. Then I was to take my dose: a half teaspoonful.

If those directions confused you a tad—like what a phone book and the prohibition of ceramic cups had to do with healing me of depression—then you can imagine what kinds of thoughts were passing through my noggin.

Still, I was desperate, so I saw this man a few more times. I bought all kinds of other stuff from him: magnesium packets, Crataegus Blend, Liquid B-Complex, Arctic Cod Liver Oil, and lots of Himalayan Goji Juice. With practically no guidance or instruction, I gobbled up as many supplements and herbs and minerals and homeopathic remedies as he was willing to sell me, which could have stocked five wellness centers for a year.

In retrospect, of course—because desperation so often acts as a blindfold—I see that my vitamin orgy was probably as dangerous as all the SSRIs, antipsychotics, and sedatives I was taking courtesy of Pharma King. These "natural" supplements have potential for harm when taken in large doses—and if you haven't picked up on this already, I struggle with that whole moderation concept. Even in modest doses, they can be hazardous when taken in combination with prescription drugs, or in combination with each other, and especially with niacin, folic acid, calcium, magnesium, iron, zinc, and vitamins A to K.

Here's the thing: we don't know squat about so many of the supplements in the health-food aisle because, thanks to the 1994 Dietary Supplement Health and Education Act, dietary supplements and homeopathic remedies aren't required to provide premarket evidence of safety and effectiveness. In May 2006 the National Institutes of Health said this:

> The F.D.A. has insufficient resources and legislative authority to require specific safety data from dietary supplement manufacturers or distributors before or after their products are made available to the public. . . . The constraints imposed on F.D.A. . . . make it difficult for the health of the American public to be adequately protected.

The last $200 I dropped on the naturopath was a packet in which I was to send my urine away, to NeuroScience, to determine my neurotransmitter levels. That, my Hopkins doctor would later tell me, was not a smart use of my money.

As if I wasn't confused enough already, wasting money needlessly in my pursuit of sanity, I also hired a medical intuitive—the politically correct term for *psychic*—who I hoped could tell me the source of my depression in an hour-and-a-half phone session.

"Tell me about your birth," she asked me.

"You mean when my mom had me?"

"Yes."

"Well, her doctor was going on vacation, so she had me induced."

"Ah. You are a Pitocin baby," she said. "That's unfortunate."

"Why?"

"Because you were forced into the world before you were ready, and therefore are always longing to go back from where you came."

"But my twin sister was forced out with me, and she's not crazy."

The conversation wasn't a total waste of $150. But I sort of wished I had used it on a fine dinner with Eric to be scheduled when my love for food returned.

To ensure that I hadn't skipped over any piece of alternative therapy that could heal me, I also tried craniosacral therapy, massage therapy, breath work, affirmation tapes, and Tibetan meditation. I kept a gratitude journal and analyzed my distorted thoughts on cognitive-behavioral worksheets; I attended support groups, did 12-step work, and wrote letters to my inner child. I read Deepak Chopra and recorded in a notebook all the coincidences that happened throughout my day so that I could chart the yellow brick road to my soul's purpose, to the place the universe was guiding me. I devoured all kinds of Buddhist literature.

I worked with a New Age doctor-guru who was helping me to wean off all my meds, even though I was still suicidal, because all the therapy, meditation, vitamins, and service work that I was going to do would more than compensate for the absence of an antidepressant and mood stabilizer in my bloodstream.

Right.

What was I thinking?

I was thinking that a morsel of Zoloft—50 mg, anyway—would hold me over until I mastered my mind and learned how to think myself out of every panic attack, manic cycle, and suicidal thought that had plagued me since Pitocin ungraciously kicked me out of the womb.

I also attended candlelight yoga every Friday evening for a year because regular yoga, according to some study I had read, can effectively raise the GABA levels (the neurotransmitter gamma-aminobutyric acid), which can improve anxiety and depression symptoms. I sought courage in warrior pose, stability in tree pose, and peace in lotus pose.

I adamantly believe in the mind-body connection, which is why I expected yoga, prayer, and meditation to heal me of my depression. I figured that if relaxation exercises and mindfulness can combat and prevent heart disease and diabetes, as studies indicate, then breath work and meditation should surely correct the distortions in my brain electrochemistry, rejuvenate nerve cell connections, and amend any structural or functional damage of this neuro-degenerative disorder. Self-loathing and suicidal ideations would disappear under my yoga mat if I said "Om" often enough.

I am one of those nerds who studies neurobiology for kicks. So I know all about recent research that has discovered the brain's neuroplasticity, its capacity to change in structure and function according to experience and thoughts. I'm cognizant of the brain's ability to reorganize itself by forming neural connections, and that our thoughts can alert those neuronal connections. And I've analyzed the collaborative works between Buddhist scholars and western psychologists, neuroscientists, and philosophers that offer methods for training the mind and cultivating compassion, the antidote to toxic emotions.

For example, there was a series of experiments awhile back con-ducted at the University of California–Los Angeles, in which Jef-frey Schwartz and colleagues applied the therapeutic potential of mindful meditation—the type practiced by Buddhist monks—to a group of patients struggling with obsessive-compulsive disorder. After ten weeks of mindfulness-based meditation, brain scans showed dramatic changes in the orbital frontal cortex, the core of the OCD circuit, similar to the effects OCD meds achieve. Schwartz calls this brain-changing activity of the mind "self-directed neuroplasticity."

The same results happened when cognitive-behavioral techniques were used to treat depression. In a specific study at the University of Toronto, fourteen depressives underwent cognitive-behavioral therapy: replacing distorted thoughts that cause unwanted feelings and behavior with positive or realistic thoughts associated with mental and physical health. Brain scans showed some interesting results.

But here's the thing: *It wasn't working for me.*

After an hour of stretching in yoga—releasing my toxic energy and peering out to the world with my "third eye"—I was as anxious as before class. Praying with Scripture and practicing Tibetan meditation didn't calm me in the way it was supposed to. My depression only worsened with each new study I read, every new attempt I made to rewire my brain, and after every comment from well-intentioned but uneducated friends that "if I only learned how to master my thoughts and control my emotions, then I wouldn't need medication, and I wouldn't be depressed."

I had already failed as a mother who couldn't be at her son's preschool Thanksgiving feast after having her car keys taken away; and a wife who couldn't accompany her husband to an office dinner without tearing up in front of his coworkers; and a writer who was losing her ability to concentrate long enough to compose a sentence. Now I was beginning to think that I had failed as a person.

Because I couldn't think myself to health, I felt like the earth's most pathetic creature, a moronic weakling. The self-empowerment preached by Caroline Myss, Deepak Chopra, and other holistic experts deceived me, contaminating me worse than Pharma King's drugs. Because back when I had been in a physically toxic state loaded up on meds, I could at least blame Pharma King or his pills. But with the New-Age, you-are-your-thoughts philosophy, and almost no medication at all, it was my own damn fault that I couldn't get it together. There was no one to curse but me.

And that made me hate me.

Each day that I couldn't redirect my thoughts and get better, my urge to die began to resurface. My suicidal plans reappeared and became more specific and intense. For months on end, my fears escalated.

This was the dialog that began to swirl inside my head as I sat, palms upward in lotus pose, at my candlelight yoga class:

One hour at a time. You can do it. Just make it to the end of class.

Then what? Do the math. I'm only thirty-five. I could live up to sixty more years. I might be less than halfway through my life. A truly frightening thought. If I had a terminal illness—cancer or some tumor—I could probably hold on a few more years. But what if God isn't merciful and makes me endure another five or six decades? Can't do it.

Stop it. God, be with me. Think positively. Life is a gift.

That's a bloody lie. Why should I say that when I don't mean it? Why did God create me if all I want to do is die? Everyone feels this way. It's just un-American to admit it. This nation is too programmed by Disney and McDonald's to be real. No one questions the attitude-of-gratitude that is force-fed to us all the time.

Where does everyone find the strength to go on? Why doesn't everyone commit suicide? Are people just better at faking happiness than I am? I am a crappy liar. That's my problem. Make-believe worlds have never appealed to me. On this side of death, anyway. Peace isn't here. It's there. I've got to get there. Now.

Stop it. Concentrate on your breath. It's speeding up. Slow down. Inhale. One. Two. Three. Four. Exhale. God, be with me. Positive thoughts. Why can't you do that? Blessings! Count them!

Ninety-nine percent of the world has it worse than me and yet they have grateful hearts. I am a spoiled brat holding all the goodies and complaining. I have no reason to feel this way. I'm a pathetic, self-absorbed creature. Maybe I am miserable because I don't do enough charity work. Life isn't meant to be enjoyed. It's about helping others. I need to volunteer more.

Uh-oh. Here I go. I can't stop the tears. Think happy thoughts. David's birth. Katherine's. Your wedding day. Some happy childhood memory. Go there. Now. God, be with me.

Those memories don't matter anymore. I'm not the person I was and I never will be. The kids deserve a better mother, someone who can be there for them instead of crying and shaking at all their activities. David has already been affected by my erratic moods. Look at his conduct in karate yesterday. He needs a mom who can nurture him emotionally. Not a sobbing mess of a mom always worried about her next anxiety attack.

I need to do something before the kids form too many memories of their whackjob mother. If I frame my suicide as an accident, they will get over it soon enough.

Stop. Stop. Think positive. Light. God, be with me. Breathing. Slow it down.

Last time I counted I had at least twenty bottles of old prescriptions stashed away in the garage. That should be plenty to do the job. But what if it doesn't? I can't make Eric take care of a veggie his whole life. I want him to move on. He deserves better, someone who can contribute more to family life than I ever did. I'll have to combine the drugs with another method.

Harry from the psych ward told me about his plan to jump off the

Bay Bridge. That could work. But there's a chance it wouldn't take me all the way. Again, veggie world. Plus it doesn't look like an accident.

I could catch a flight to Baghdad, or show up in Kabul in a bikini.

Stop it! Stop it! Think positive. God, be with me! Why aren't you there? God! Why aren't you there?

Eric knows I'm a horrible driver. Why not crash really hard into a tree or a concrete wall or the side of a building? I could take the twenty bottles and then drive into the wall, just to make sure.

God, be with me!

Stop. Please stop. Think positive. Practice controlled breathing. God, be with me.

Got it! I'll rent a kayak, take the twenty bottles of pills, and tie weights to my ankles. My body will be swallowed up by Spa Creek. And the kids won't have too much baggage because it will look like a kayaking accident. I've got to do it soon. Before I permanently damage my two little loves. And before Eric loses too much of his heart and soul by hanging out with me. It's the right thing to do: for me, for the kids, and for Eric.

Stop. Positive thoughts. Breathing. God, be with me.

Thursday mornings I have a sitter. Springriver starts renting kayaks at 10 a.m. The weather is still warm enough.

God, be with me.

One evening, four months after I'd turned my back on the medical community and on everything I had learned about my depression in my college years, after I'd exposed myself to every New Age, holistic approach I could find and flunked Holistic Healing 101, Eric found me in our bedroom closet kneeling in child's pose, sobbing and shaking, as I breathed into a paper bag.

"What are you doing?" he asked.

"I didn't want the kids to see me this way," I explained.

"Why didn't you call me?"

"You can't come home every time it happens."

He knelt down on the maroon carpet and pulled me into him, combing my hair with his fingers. He held me so tightly that his body began to shake with mine.

"What are we going to do about this?" he asked.

"It's my fault. I'm not strong enough. Or not disciplined enough. I'm trying to train my thoughts. I'm trying so hard. But I can't stop thinking about all the ways I could kill myself."

"This approach isn't working, Therese. Look at you. . . . I think we'd better work with a traditional psychiatrist, find a new doctor."

"I've read the studies, Eric," I lashed back. "The brain is plastic and I can change its patterns through meditation and breath work. I should be able to do this. To alter my mood by changing my thoughts."

He continued to comb my hair behind my ears and pulled me in tighter still.

"Therese, when I was in the fourth grade I watched a documentary one night about Uri Geller, the world's most famous paranormalist. He was able to bend a spoon with his thoughts. For two weeks I sat down with a spoon at the kitchen table, trying to do the same. I finally gave up, put the spoon back in the silverware drawer, and ran out to play with my friends."

He paused for a minute.

"You've been staring at that spoon a long time."

"But if I label myself as a manic depressive, I'm limiting myself on what I have the power to do and the freedom to be."

I was referring to a piece I had just read by Rachel Naomi Remen. She wrote:

> A label is a mask life wears. Labeling sets up an expectation of life that is often so compelling we can no longer see things as they really are. . . . In my experience, a diagnosis

is an opinion and not a prediction. What would it be like if more people allowed for the presence of the unknown, and accepted the words of their medical experts in the same way? The diagnosis is cancer. What that will mean remains to be seen.

"I can't be a caretaker my whole life, Therese."

He was right. He had already taken the equivalent of three months off of work to care for me and the kids. And we had shelled out more than fifteen thousand dollars in doctors' fees, prescriptions, psychics, and Chinese herbs.

"Your quality of life can be better," he continued. "Our quality of life can be better. Let's go to Johns Hopkins. They have a team of top-notch doctors."

"They'll throw out a bunch of diagnoses and pump me full of meds. . . . I can't do that again, Eric. I can't go back there. I can't let doctors poison me again."

He was growing impatient and agitated. Clearly my condition had pushed him to his threshold and beyond, and I couldn't help feeling guilty, horribly guilty, for putting our family through this.

He waited for a while, just holding me, as I shook.

"Therese, I can't keep on going into the office petrified that when I walk through the door in the evening I'm going to find you dead." His voice cracked and he began to cry.

"Please. . . . Do this for me," he said.

There was silence for a long while.

"I'll go," I said. "I'll go."

They Just Don't Get It

I used to resent my New Age friends for what I perceived to be selfish acts on their parts—using my suicidal days as opportunities to promote their philosophies. But now I know they were only responding with love. They were scared, too, and offered to me the tools and techniques that had worked for them.

When Liz encouraged me to train my mind without drugs—to reach inside myself for the strength and the discipline to do it without the crutch of medication—she spoke with no understanding of what it's like to have your survival instinct completely dead, to have 99 percent of your energy going toward not pursuing one of five ways to kill yourself.

Then again, how can you make a person who has never wanted to die appreciate the terrifying power of suicidal thoughts?

It's like being famished, incredibly hungry at a cocktail party, and trays of crab balls, brie cheese, stuffed mushrooms, and mini chocolate torts keep coming by. But you know what looks so good is really poison. So you try to distract yourself from your hunger as best you can—by starting a shallow conversation with someone about his precocious two-year-old who can already read, or hanging out by the window, people watching. But your stomach rumbles again. And more trays come by. You don't know how much longer you can take it, until you say "To hell with it," and reach for the crab ball.

Or, here's a better analogy: It's like you are desperately lonely and holding a cell phone. You only want to call your ex-boyfriend, the love of your life who was actually abusive and destroying you. But you wake up the next morning and thank the Lord in heaven you didn't do it.

I felt like that for five hundred days, or twelve thousand hours, with the phone in my hand—wanting so badly to dial the number.

Thank God I called my mom instead.

Daily.

Having experienced similar anguish after my dad left, she was one of the few people who got my depression.

I called her in tears one day, when a friend went on a tirade against antidepressants, describing how they suppressed a person's emotions and insinuating that I'd do well to pitch the happy pills and tough it out like the rest of humanity.

"No one understands, Mom," I said. "You and Eric. That's it. And Michelle, Ann, and Mike. Everyone else thinks I'm weak for joining the droves of Americans on Prozac."

"Who cares?" she asked. "Why do you need their approval?"

"Because I'm not weak and it's unfair to be labeled that way," I explained.

"I don't think you're weak. Eric doesn't. And you have several friends who believe in you. If you don't want to be constantly frustrated I suggest you lower your expectations. Assume that people won't understand and you'll be less disappointed when they don't."

She was right. I expected my friends Sue, Liz, and everyone else to know what severe depression felt like. Just as seasoned parents say "Just you wait!" to the pregnant lady in front of them at the checkout line, a person can't begin to appreciate the harrowing darkness of depression unless she's been there.

William Styron wrote his memoir, *Darkness Visible*, as a response to the public's reaction to the suicide of Primo Levi, the Italian-Jewish writer and chemist who had survived the Holocaust. The scholars who admired Levi wondered how he could have endured years of torture by the Nazis yet break under depression.

"The pain of severe depression is quite unimaginable to those who have not suffered it," Styron wrote. "To the tragic legion who are compelled to destroy themselves there should be no more reproof attached than to the victims of terminal cancer."

Like Styron, I was both enraged and saddened by the reactions of friends and family. They were shocked to hear that two doctors sliced me open—before full anesthesia kicked in—to save little David's life in an emergency C-section. Yet when I voiced the desperation of depression—which made the knife cut feel like a knee scratch—they often brushed it off, as if I were whining to win some undeserved sympathy votes. If my New Age friends saw me in a wheelchair, with two arm casts and two leg casts, what would they say? *For crying out loud, why did you think yourself into that mess? Now count your blessings and snap out of it!*

That's exactly what I heard from across the table at lunch every time they suggested I try another Chinese herb or mind-control seminar. I was empty-handed when it came to lab results and X-rays—that is, until an MRI did show a tumor in my pituitary gland. All they had to go on was my creative story about how a bunch of neurotransmitters in my brain were lost and, like my stepfather, refused to ask for directions—plus the structural and functional disruption of brain cells (i.e., a neural-circuit blowout) that neurobiologists are discovering happens with depression.

I'm finally reaching a point where I don't internalize all the judgments cast my way with regard to how I have decided to treat my depression. The longer I am well, the less I care about converting the world to my own health philosophies. And the more I share my story with depressives who understand every word I say and hear their tales of triumph over this beast, the more I am able to simply shrug and laugh at an offensive comment about crazies who take meds, then say under my breath, "They just don't get it."

Chapter Eight

The Land of Oz

My Happy Ending

In general, I find happy endings annoying (there is way too much Disney in our house), so I often forget to tell mine. I usually don't go beyond the part of my story where I'm shaking and crying, and my jeans are hanging from my hip bones because I'm so skinny, and I'm painting an ugly plaque of the Serenity Prayer during my session of occupational therapy at the Laurel Regional psych ward as the nurses check in the guy who just had his stomach pumped after chugging down a gallon of Tide laundry detergent because his pregnant girlfriend left him for Dr. Phil. Okay, the Dr. Phil thing isn't true.

That's so much more interesting, no? And, as a writer, I find it's just better material, plain and simple.

But some Beyond Blue readers have asked me for an honest, straightforward conclusion to my stories from inside the psych ward. They are like Dr. Evil in *Austin Powers*: "Come on, Therese, throw us a friggin' bone (of hope)."

. . .

Eric and I arrived at the campus of Johns Hopkins Hospital the morning of my psychiatric consultation, much as Dorothy and her friends finally made it to the Emerald City in *The Wizard of Oz*. Like the scarecrow, I wanted a new brain. Forget about a heart and courage. I wanted to be able to hold a spoon of Cheerios steadily with my hand and bring it to my mouth without effort. I wished to be able to taste it, to swallow it, and to enjoy it. I desired to eat my breakfast with orange juice and coffee and to be able to fetch both of those things without deteriorating into tears and panic—hit with a half-dozen suicidal thoughts—before I reached the refrigerator and coffeemaker.

Like Dorothy and her pair of red slippers, Eric would have done just about anything to go "home": to the happy place in our marriage when I laughed at his jokes and found humor in dumb stuff; back when I could plan fun play dates for the kids and be able to shuttle David to karate practice and Katherine to her Halloween party without losing control of the car because my shaking hands, in a panic attack, could no longer clutch the steering wheel; to be confident and creative enough to organize adventures to the pumpkin patch, instead of having to be rescued from them, an emotional wreck of a mom waiting to be bailed out by her husband.

As we circled the campus trying to find the right building, Eric held my trembling arm and guided my steps just as I had done for my legally blind mom two years earlier. I was as frail and fragile as my mom had been when the two of us made the pilgrimage to Hopkins, the eye mecca of the world, hoping for a miracle for her after she had been diagnosed with blepharospasm, a neurological eye disorder that causes involuntary facial movements like blinking. Like me with my mood disorder, my mom was tired of doctor hopping, trying any and all suggestions doled from family and friends, and experimenting with all sorts of alternative approaches. Hopkins was her last chance.

But the wizard was a weasel.

"I'm sorry," said Dr. F on that cold rainy morning. He spoke with absolutely no expression on his face. "What you have is a wretched disorder and there's nothing I can do about it."

As we entered the garage, my mom lit up a cigarette and cried harder than I've ever seen her cry.

We departed the city of Oz disillusioned.

Now it was my turn to wish. Would the doctors say the same thing to me? I thought to myself, as Eric and I looked for the right building on the day my miracle began. Or worse, would they give me false hope, like Pharma King did when he promised me that the newer antipsychotics would not only relieve my depression but deliver me to a stable, peaceful place I had not yet experienced—that modern medicine was like technology, on our side, and it was just a matter of finding and fine-tuning the right cocktail? Pharma King had claimed that utopia was just over the rainbow, so I waited and waited and waited. And with every month and each new medication combination I deteriorated into a toxic, semidelusional mess.

I tried not to think about all the prescriptions the Hopkins doctors were going to hand me—for SSRIs, antipsychotics, and tranquilizers. But every paranoia I had about medication was validated in the O magazine article Liz had handed me as Eric and I headed out the door that morning.

The piece, entitled "Valley of the Dulls: Taking Antidepressants," included several interviews with people who claimed that antidepressants zapped their creativity, sex drive, passion, cognitive ability, and zest for life. It was the perfect article for a hypersensitive professional worrier on her way to a psychiatric evaluation with a team of brain experts.

What is going to make this meeting any different than all the others? I wondered. *Nothing. Do I really think this group of professionals knows more than the six who have already seen me, that they'll be able to find the missing link to my health that the others failed to catch? No. And what if these people can't fix me? Then no one can.* That last thought terrified me the most.

Fear consumed me.

Until I saw Jesus.

In the lobby of Hopkins's Billings Administration Building was a ten-and-a-half-foot tall marble statue of Jesus, his arms extended toward those in desperate need of healing. The inscription, written in capital letters on the pedestal, read: "Come unto me all ye that are weary and heavy laden, and I will give you rest."

I stood in front of Jesus for a while, tempted to touch his robe like the hemorrhaging woman who got her miracle in the gospels of Mark and Luke. She had bled for twelve years, "had endured much under many physicians, and had spent all that she had; and she was no better" (Mark 5:26). Just by touching the hem of Jesus' cloak, this ailing woman was healed of her disease, because her faith was so great.

"I believe, Jesus," I said to the statue, imagining myself touching the hem of Jesus' real robe, "I believe."

And I wept at his feet.

Eric and I finally found the Meyer Building and Johns Hopkins's Department of Psychiatry and Behavioral Sciences, which felt somewhat magical to me, even in its sterile environment. It is home to Kay Redfield Jamison, one of the foremost authorities on manic depression. Her riveting memoir, *An Unquiet Mind*, was the first book I ever read on the subject. I wept at certain passages, because for the first time in my life I felt as though someone understood me. Really understood me. Her incisive writing helped me to place certain conversations and memories in undergraduate and graduate school into their proper context of illness. She wrote:

> My thinking, far from being clearer than a crystal, was tortuous. I would read the same passage over and over

again only to realize that I had no memory at all for what I just had read. Each book or poem I picked up was the same way. Incomprehensible. Nothing made sense. I could not begin to follow the material presented in my classes, and I would find myself staring out the window with no idea of what was going on around me. It was very frightening.

I remember crying to my senior thesis adviser about my inability to read and retain information. I told him that no matter how hard I studied or how much time I dedicated to my assignments, the words were not getting through. I hated Karl Rahner and Kierkegaard for making me feel so stupid.

At the time I begged my higher power to grant me one-fourth of the brain of my best friend, Beatriz, our class's valedictorian at Saint Mary's, who spoke seven languages and could read ten. I didn't know that at least part of bipolar disorder, according to psychiatrists like Dean MacKinnon, comes from a disorder in adaptation—a disorder in emotional learning—and therefore affects cognitive performance and learning aptitudes. MacKinnon argues that because of a bipolar's failure in conditioning (a basic kind of learning), at times of stress or change "people with bipolar disorder can't maintain that sort of learning."

All I knew was that my mind was turning on me, exactly as it did for Jamison:

> I was used to my mind being my best friend; of carrying on endless conversations within my head; of having a built-in source of laughter or analytic thought to rescue me from boring or painful surroundings. I counted upon my mind's acuity, interest, and loyalty as a matter of course. Now, all of a sudden, my mind had turned on me: it mocked me

for my vapid enthusiasms; it laughed at all of my foolish plans; it no longer found anything interesting or enjoyable or worthwhile. It was incapable of concentrated thought and turned time and again to the subject of death: I was going to die, what difference did anything make? Life's run was only a short and meaningless one, why live?

From the perspective of both healer and healed (Jamison too suffers from bipolar disorder), this author convinced me that having a mental illness didn't necessarily mean the end of creative thinking and everything intellectual, a termination of all success—that "tumultuousness, if coupled to discipline and a cool mind, is not such a bad sort of thing." Sensitivity and volatile moods had made heroes out of Abraham Lincoln, Winston Churchill, William Styron, Emily Dickinson, and Patty Duke.

Maybe there was hope for me.

As we sat in the waiting room outside the small offices of Johns Hopkins's brain hub, Eric and I read some of the medical newsletters and articles made available to patients. I read about the encouraging research into the genetics of mood disorders: that linkage studies of bipolar disorder have found evidence for susceptibility genes on certain chromosomes, and that psychiatric geneticists have located and identified genes associated with schizophrenia. I learned that more than twenty studies suggest that the hippocampus—the part of the brain's limbic system responsible for human emotion—is smaller in patients with major depression than in those without the illness (by approximately 10 percent), and that the longer a depression goes untreated, the more brain loss there is.

All this meant was that I might soon be able to show my New Age friends and other doubting Thomases proof of my brain disease.

After an intense two-hour evaluation, Dr. Milena Hruby Smith left us to meet Dr. Karen Swartz, director of clinical programs at the Johns Hopkins Mood Disorders Center. Then Eric and I were asked to join both of them.

"Dr. Smith has shared with me all the information," said Dr. Swartz. "And I support her judgment that Mrs. Borchard should be admitted into our inpatient program as soon as possible."

Oh God, no, I thought. No, not that. Please not that. Not the rubber chicken, hourly group therapy, psychotic women yelling profanities down the hall, mentally disabled teenagers hitting on me as I try to paint a pathetic birdhouse in occupational therapy, no fresh air or sunlight.

Committing myself to the psych ward a second time, in my mind, meant that I was officially relinquishing any self-respect or self-confidence I had going into this evaluation.

Annapolis is small. Rumors spread like California wildfires in August. When word got out the first time that I had been hospitalized for a mental breakdown, I avoided neighborhood parks, preschool fund-raisers, and Giant Food at rush hour. Humiliated by my hospital stay, I couldn't face the folks who would wave a finger in my face and say: "If only you ate organically, or went to yoga more, or prayed more faithfully, or could move beyond your childhood crap—if only you were a stronger person." If I returned to the hospital that would mean I had joined the group of regulars, the real crazies that were on disability because they couldn't handle any kind of responsibility or job.

The doctors could immediately sense my unease, so they directed their argument primarily toward Eric.

"It's like this," Dr. Swartz began to explain. "Therese has been wearing a backpack of heavy rocks for over a year. Almost all of her energy has been directed toward staying alive and not pursing a path of suicide."

I started to cry.

"Any responsibilities on top of that only compound her weight and make it that much more difficult to improve."

A torrent of tears was now running down my cheeks. As Brooke Shields says, down came the rain—or hail, more like it. Kleenex was useless.

"We want to give her three or four days in a safe setting where she doesn't have to worry about not harming herself. That rest will assist her recovery. If she is admitted inpatient, we can also begin to treat her aggressively with new medications, which will expedite the process. She'll feel better sooner."

Is this the truth? Or are they imitating Pharma King with his better-than-better prediction? I wondered.

Eric turned to me. "Let's do it, Therese."

"The kids?"

"I can handle it. This is more important."

I stayed. And I discovered a few months later that those two women were telling the truth. The doctors at Oz know their stuff.

Dr. Smith became my seventh and hopefully last psychiatrist. A wise and insightful doctor, she not only knew her meds and their side effects, she made an effort to identify the strengths of her patients and helped them to use those strengths to paddle toward recovery.

Sensing my skepticism of her manic-depression diagnosis and how my quest for understanding could very well hurt my progress, she suggested I not read so many opinions on depression until I reached a more stable place.

That was after several weeks of coming into her office with another book and another paragraph that contradicted what she and the other Hopkins doctors were saying.

For example, one week I brought in Michael D. Yapko's book *Breaking the Patterns of Depression*. My copy was marked to page fourteen, which read:

> Many doctors suggest depression is caused by a "chemical imbalance in the brain," but there is no reliable test to identify any such imbalance. It is simply assumed to exist whenever someone is depressed. Then, if a person responds well to antidepressant medication, it is taken as confirming evidence. Such a conclusion is not fully justified, however, because mood-altering drugs can have an effect even when there is no "chemical imbalance."

"Is that true?" I asked Dr. Smith.

"No. If antidepressants made everyone feel better they would be sold on the streets along with Adderall and other stimulants."

Another week I showed up in tears with a copy of M. Scott Peck's *The Road Less Traveled* tucked under my arm.

"I'm afraid I'm not getting to the core of my problem," I explained. "What if my depression is really a result of childhood issues I have yet to resolve or some problem that I'm not facing? M. Scott Peck says that it is almost impossible to recover from a past of abandonment, and that being nurtured and feeling secure in those early years are the cornerstone of mental health. I wonder how my parents' divorce and my mom's subsequent depression factor into all of this.

"I mean, listen to this. . . . 'When [self-discipline and consistent, genuine caring] have not been proffered by one's parents, it is possible to acquire them from other sources, but in that case the process of their acquisition is invariably an uphill struggle, often of lifelong duration and often unsuccessful.'

"Did you hear that? Often unsuccessful!"

She smiled. "These books that you keep bringing in weren't written for people like you who are always examining themselves under a microscope and are prone to self-doubt. They are meant for people who live a little on the surface, who could benefit from some self-scrutiny."

"But should I be doing anything more than I am? Addressing a certain issue in therapy? Working on any specific cognitive-behavioral worksheet? Doing some breathing exercise? Going to yoga more?"

She smirked.

And I got it.

Trying too hard was precisely my problem. It was the "mind over spoon" issue again. In my mind, I was failing because I couldn't think myself to perfect health. I couldn't do it all myself.

Dr. Smith salvaged the last crumb of my self-esteem with this compassionate statement: "Mindful meditation, yoga, and cognitive-behavioral therapy are extremely helpful for people with mild to moderate depression. But they don't work for people such as yourself who are suicidal or severely depressed."

Her advice was grounded in neuroscience.

One research study at the University of Wisconsin–Madison, in particular, used high-definition brain imaging to reveal a breakdown in the emotional processing that impairs the depressive's ability to suppress negative emotions. In fact, the more effort that depressives put into reframing thoughts—the harder they tried to think positive—the more activation there was in the amygdala, regarded by neurobiologists as a person's "fear center." Says Tom Johnstone, PhD, the lead study author at the University of Wisconsin:

> Healthy individuals putting more cognitive effort into [reframing the content] get a bigger payoff in terms of decreasing activity in the brain's emotional response

centers. In the depressed individuals, you find the exact opposite.

And then Dr. Smith asked me this: If I had been in a terrible automobile accident would I be so hard on myself?

"If you were in a wheelchair with casts on each of your limbs," she said, "would you beat yourself up for not healing yourself with your thoughts? For not thinking yourself into perfect condition?"

Of course not.

When I injured my knee while training for a marathon, I didn't expect myself to visualize my tendonitis away so that I could run. I dropped out of the race to rest my joints and muscles so I wouldn't further damage them.

Yet I expected myself to think away my mood disorder, which involved a disease in my brain—an organ just like my heart, lungs, and kidneys.

"What's most important is to find a medication combination that works so that you can be able to do all that other stuff to feel even better," she said. "I will give you a list of books you should read if you want to study depression. Until you feel stronger, I suggest you stay away from the type of self-help literature you have brought in, because those texts can do further damage if read in a very depressed state."

That became my New Year's resolution: to become more close-minded. To ignore the judgments and suggestions and advice that the world has to offer on depression and just focus on material sanctioned by the doctors of Oz.

Dr. Smith was the first psychiatrist I truly trusted. My previous six hadn't been a good fit, and I was, well, beginning to think it was me. Her philosophy was a perfect match to mine: she was conservative with meds, wanting to exhaust the benefits of personal therapy, cognitive-behavioral therapy, exercise, light therapy, nutrition, regular sleep, and a host of other tools alongside drugs. That impressed me because I was committed to treating my depression in a holistic way, using anything and everything that would help me.

During the first rocky weeks after I was discharged from the inpatient program, when she was trying a new combination of meds, she told me to rely on my family, my friends, and my faith—that I might feel worse before I feel better—because she didn't want to adjust the meds until we gave them at least six weeks to work. That delighted me even more, given Pharma King's practically daily modifications.

After six or seven months on medication combination 23— Lithium, Nortriptyline, and Zoloft—I reached some semblance of stability. The knot in my stomach unraveled—that is, without large quantities of Valium. I stopped shaking—without large quantities of Valium. My senses returned, the most important being taste, of course. And my mornings were no longer scary. The first question I asked myself upon waking was no longer: *How am I going to make it through the day?* I began to notice the details again—the freckle on Katherine's right butt cheek, David's red highlights, my gray hair coming in.

Something must have happened the moment I wept at Jesus' feet in the lobby of the administration building at Hopkins, when I told the holy guy that I really did believe in miracles and I was in desperate need of one.

Because eventually I got mine.

Dear Kate: It Will Get Better

I wrote the following letter to Kate, a despondent reader on Beyond Blue, who was so buried in the Black Hole that she could see nothing but darkness.

Dear Kate,

You say that no one can understand your despair. I have no doubt you feel completely alone in your battle. But I'm pretty sure a few people have known similar pain.

I, for one, recognized your plea to God: "Why did you create me if all I want to do is die?" I asked that same question plus a few fillers for at least 18 months. I pounded my fists on my bedroom floor with such rage that I nearly fractured my wrists, and I threw books like What Happy People Know *and* Authentic Happiness *over the banister in a temper-tantrum.*

That was a good sign. It meant I hadn't given up. Like you. I was still in the game. Ticked off, but still playing.

I'm going to sound like a cross between cheesy motivational speaker Anthony Robbins and New Age guru Deepak Chopra with this directive, but you have to tap the life force within you. It's there. And call on your Creator. Cuss him out. Yell at him. Say whatever you want. But don't stop talking. Because as long as you are saying something, you're communicating, and that means you are in a relationship with him. He can't give up on you.

You know those 12 steps I talk about? Scrap them. Just do this: hang in there. Because this really will pass. Even if you never find the exact right cocktail or doctor or support group. It will get better. And you will be there to reach out to some young Kate along the way, maybe a relative or a friend or maybe a stranger, and you'll convince her to stay, too, because you're starting to have a little fun.

My prayers are with you, and I wish you much peace.

Therese

Chapter Nine

Exuberance

What's Underneath the Bumps

Although we weren't allowed to roast marshmallows in the psych ward of Johns Hopkins, there were many campfire moments, where we sat in a circle sharing some of our most intimate memories, stories, hopes, and fears that, along with a power failure in the left part of the prefrontal cortex, had our minds gripped by anxiety and depression.

One group therapy session that I remember well at Camp Psych Ward was the hour our Girl Scout leader, I mean psych unit nurse, told us to recall a few of our favorite activities. Just like Julie Andrews does in *The Sound of Music*, except that Andrews sticks to nouns, and the nurse wanted verbs.

"I know it's difficult to think about that right now when you are so depressed," she said. "But you will enjoy those things again. I promise you. You will enjoy them again."

I thought about four things that I love to do—diversions that help me to decompress when I'm stressed out: playing at the downtown park with Katherine and David, riding my bike along the Severn River, running through the stunning campus of the Naval Academy, and kayaking in Spa Creek with David.

I shared those with the group and then listened to what kind of stuff energized my fellow campers: family picnics, murder mystery novels, journal writing, crossword puzzles and coffee, movies and popcorn, long hikes through the woods, mountain biking, chess, video games, surfing the Internet, and so on.

It was all very interesting. But I didn't believe the nurse for a second.

Because for months and more months, I had been forcing myself to do those things I loved, and I still wanted to die. Even when I made myself accept an invitation to ride my bike with friends, I continued to cry along the way because the suicidal thoughts stalked me, pestering me like a pushy fiancé to nail down a specific date and plan.

Still, I took the kids to the park. I rode my bike. I ran. Obsessing about death and crying most of the time.

But then one day I ran six miles without tears. Two weeks later I could push Katherine in the baby swing at the park without shaking. Three weeks after that I biked the Baltimore-Annapolis trail and made only one suicidal plan instead of my average of six.

In hindsight I suspect this is what was happening: My bumps were growing wings, so that they could fly away.

That's Katherine's theory.

When bumps go away, that means they have sprouted wings and have taken off, into the sky.

About the same time as I overheard my three-year-old biologist's sophisticated explanation of how a bulge dissipates, I took David kayaking. We explored all the little fingers and waterways of Spa Creek, two curious travelers on a sea expedition.

"Look, David!" I said. "It's a water turtle!" We immediately paddled up to it, which was a bad idea, because upon getting a closer look, I saw that it was dead. So I lied to my boy: "No he's not dead, he's just taking a nap, the tired little fella."

At that point I could have easily shifted into negative

thinking—fretting about the polluted Chesapeake Bay, which is too toxic for turtles and fish to thrive. But I didn't. I rested my paddle on my lap, took in the gorgeous view of our town, and let the breeze play with my hair. I was tempted to kneel on the front of the kayak, stretch my arms out wide, raise my 38B chest to the sun, and yell "King of the World!"

I thought to myself in that moment: "Oh . . . my . . . God . . . I'm happy!"

I immediately remembered that group therapy session at Johns Hopkins, when the bubbly nurse promised us that we would positively and absolutely enjoy our favorite things again. In other words, our bumps would eventually grow wings and fly away.

Recovery from severe depression is much like the metamorphosis of a caterpillar to a butterfly.

Only in struggling to emerge from a small hole in the cocoon does a butterfly form wings strong enough to fly. As she squeezes out of that tiny space, the liquids inside her body cavity are pushed into the tiny capillaries in the wings, where they harden. Should you try to help a butterfly by tearing open the cocoon, the poor thing won't sprout wings. Or if she does, they would be too weak to fly.

Consider these words by Nikos Kazantzakis in *Zorba the Greek*:

> I remembered one morning when I discovered a cocoon in the bark of a tree, just as a butterfly was making a hole in its case and preparing to come out. I waited a while, but it was too long appearing and I was impatient. I bent over it and breathed on it to warm it. I warmed it as quickly as I could and the miracle began to happen

before my eyes, faster than life. The case opened, the
butterfly started slowly crawling out and I shall never
forget my horror when I saw how its wings were folded
back and crumpled; the wretched butterfly tried with its
whole trembling body to unfold them. Bending over it,
I tried to help it with my breath. In vain. It needed to
be hatched out patiently and the unfolding of the wings
should be a gradual process in the sun. Now it was too
late. My breath had forced the butterfly to appear, all
crumpled, before its time. It struggled desperately and, a
few seconds later, died in the palm of my hand.

That little body is, I do believe, the greatest weight
I have on my conscience. For I realize today that it is a
mortal sin to violate the great laws of nature. We should
not hurry, we should not be impatient, but we should confidently obey the eternal rhythm.

Butterflies are stronger and more beautiful than caterpillars as a
result of their struggle. In my dark night, I became a more loving,
forgiving, and empathetic person because, as Kahlil Gibran writes
in *The Prophet*, "Your pain is the breaking of the shell that encloses
your understanding. Even as the stone of the fruit must break, that
its heart may stand in the sun, so must you know pain."

I wouldn't go so far as to thank God for my brain disease, just
as I wouldn't praise the benevolent Creator for delegating that
whole childbirth thing to women, therefore blessing the female
gender with all the gifts that come with carrying and giving birth
to babes: saggy breasts, pituitary problems, endocrine complications, dead libidos, stretch marks, torn abdomen tissue, enlarged
feet, and thirty extra pounds.

But, because of my nightmare, I have learned some coping skills that have come in handy not only in living with extreme moodiness and anxiety, but also in toilet training my kids, being a loving wife during PMS, and respecting preschool administrators who feel that Easter deserves two weeks of vacation.

When a manic depressive, in particular, emerges from her chrysalis to take flight, she can become what you call *exuberant*, the title of Kay Redfield Jamison's book, *Exuberance: The Passion for Life*. Exuberance, not mania, is the other face of depression. Jamison writes:

> The infectious energies of exuberance that proclaim and disperse much of what is marvelous in life. Exuberance carries us places we would not otherwise go—across the savannah, to the moon, into the imagination—and if we ourselves are not so exuberant we will, caught up in the contagious joy of those who are, be inclined collectively to go yonder.

I think that paragraph explains why Eric has kept me around. My manic-depression with all its gusty winds propelled our family into Dante's inferno for more months than I care to remember, but the energy of its exuberance—which "spreads upward and outward, like pollen toted by dancing bees," says Jamison—reaps its own kind of delight and bestows life with a well-deserved meaning and adventure in a way boredom and mental stability can't.

I am, at last, beginning to appreciate my precious pearl produced in the gritty irritation of depression's shell. I have begun the "ascent of the poet," as William Styron describes, "trudging upward and upward out of hell's black depths and at last emerging into what he saw as 'the shining world.'" Styron claims that

"whoever has been restored to health has almost always been restored to the capacity for serenity and joy."

I agree.

Because the exuberance was always there—with the depression.

It was just hiding underneath the bumps.

Part II

Beyond Blue

Or At Least Headed That Way

Chapter Ten

No, Really, I'm Not Making It Up

Depression Is a Brain Disease

A reader once remarked on Beyond Blue that depression is the loneliest of all illnesses because of the stigma associated with it.

I agree.

If I collected a nickel for every uninformed statement I've heard about mental illness, I could afford my own psych ward—an entire wing of a hospital.

Here are some of my favorites:

"People with mental illness are not the only ones who wake up with heavy things on their minds. The difference is that some of us acknowledge that our mood might not be good or productive and move on."

"When you learn how to master your thoughts and control your emotions, you won't need medication. Ditch the label of *manic depression* and train your mind to believe it's possible to reprogram your thinking, because it is."

"You obviously have issues you haven't addressed. Once you get to the core of your anxiety and depression—once you get to your unconscious issues—you will be free."

"You were born with everything you need to get better."

These are all ways of saying one thing: that depressives are at fault for their disease.

Up until two years ago—when I started studying the subject of depression and bipolar disorder like a kid in med school afraid to flunk his exams—I couldn't relinquish the possibility that I had caused my own bipolar disorder. And because of that lingering probability, I was embarrassed by my illness and didn't speak openly about it.

When I started to work with Dr. Smith, I began to read all the research—the latest studies on the genetics and treatment of mood disorders—disseminated from Hopkins's Department of Psychiatry. I learned that depression and bipolar disorder are more than imbalances of neurotransmitters—serotonin, norepinephrine, and dopamine—chemicals that bridge the synaptic clefts and pass messages to each other. These diseases are the result of organic changes in specific areas of the brain, especially in the limbic system, a ring of structures that form the brain's emotional center, including the cerebral cortex, thalamus, hypothalamus, and hippocampus.

In his book *Against Depression*, Dr. Peter D. Kramer, professor of psychiatry at Brown University, provides an overview of research studies that sketch out the effect of stress hormones in the prefrontal cortex of the brain. Based on a survey of cutting-edge medical research, he believes that it's the devastation in the amygdala and hippocampus regions—the significant cell death and shrinkage, and the diminished capacity for nerve generation—that contributes to fragile moods. "The longer the episode [of depression]," he writes, "the greater the anatomical disorder. To work with depression is to combat a disease that harms patients' nerve pathways day by day."

Kramer is trying to use his synthesis of research to change attitudes among psychiatrists and patients.

"Psychiatrists have learned that depression is progressive, and there is widespread agreement that we need to interrupt it very promptly and decisively to prevent further deterioration," he writes. From a public health perspective, he believes that "depression is the most devastating disease known to mankind."

There are psychiatrists and neurologists like Helen S. Mayberg, MD, professor of psychiatry and neurology at Emory University School of Medicine in Atlanta, Georgia, who are using brain-mapping techniques to view brain activity and how those functions affect our emotions.

"Thanks to refinements in brain-imaging technologies (higher resolution in PET scans and MRIs), scientists now know that there are regional patterns of brain activity—differences in specific circuits of the brain—that distinguish depressed people from nondepressed people," she writes in an in-depth report in the October 2006 issue of *The Johns Hopkins Depression and Anxiety Bulletin.*

Mayberg sees this neurological perspective—focusing on specific brain circuits—as a new way of understanding depression, which coupled with a biochemical approach can lead to more targeted treatments.

The research into the genetics of mood disorders continues to pinpoint the genes that may predispose individuals and families to depression and bipolar disorder. There has been remarkable success in locating and identifying genes associated with schizophrenia and, more recently, with obsessive-compulsive disorder. Researchers have confirmed a role for the gene G72/G30, located on chromosome 13q, in some families with bipolar disorder, and also evidence for susceptibility genes on chromosome 18q and 22q.

Most recently, with genetic studies on families with major depression disorder, psychiatric geneticists like James Potash, MD, have been able to mark a narrow area on chromosome 15 as having a tie to depression. Says Potash, "For the first time, we have the potential to understand the truth about what sets depression in motion."

Moreover, researchers are beginning to see what a genetic predisposition to depression actually looks like. For example, the National Institute of Mental Health conducted a compelling study involving a gene known as the serotonin transporter gene. Further studies will point to biochemical pathways of disease and could lead to development of new medications to alter those pathways.

But even as all the genetic and structural information is interesting and helpful, the far more convincing data for the biological basis of mental illness, according to my psychiatrist and other doctors, is the natural history of these diseases.

"It didn't take us finding the cellular basis of HIV or cancer or tuberculosis to convince us that these were diseases," Dr. Smith explained to me recently. "It was the stereotypical nature of their symptoms and natural history." So why should it take fancy science to convince people that mental illnesses are biological diseases?

Interestingly enough, one hundred years ago tuberculosis was perceived in much the same way as depression is today. It was an illness that "signified refinement," Peter Kramer explains, containing a "measure of erotic appeal." But that diminished as science helped identify the origins of the illness and as treatment became possible and then routine. "Depression may follow the same path," writes Kramer. "As it does, we may find that heroic melancholy is no more."

Even if depressives aren't as fascinated by the biological basis of their condition as I am, they should know this: *Depression is an organic brain disorder.* As Kramer succinctly states, "Depression is not a perspective. It is a disease."

End of story.

But publicly professing that mood disorders are legitimate illnesses in our society and culture is received *almost* as well as the pushy pamphlets the Jehovah's Witnesses leave at our doors if we were lucky enough to dodge their visit. One conversation with a health-care insurance representative will have you believing that mental illnesses are much like imaginary mermaid friends—*not real.* Psychiatric conditions happen to people who can't deal with life's hard knocks, who are stuck in traumatic childhoods, who are too stupid to know what they want and too cowardly to go after it.

They are part of a make-believe world invented to get attention.

I wasn't surprised the other day, while making an appointment with a pediatric behavioral specialist for David, to get this answer when I asked the receptionist if the doctor took insurance: "It depends on the diagnosis. If it's a physical condition, most insurances will cover it. If it's mental, they won't."

Two years ago when I tried the half dozen sessions of acupuncture, Dr. P asked me in his broken English, "Do you have sore back?"

"No."

"Sore neck?"

"No."

"Tight shoulders, yes?"

"No."

"Insurance not pay for depression. You have sore back?"

The Catholic in me couldn't lie, so I forked over the eighty bucks each week until I got a sore neck thinking about how I was going to pay Dr. P.

It left me thinking: How can we ask people to ditch the stigma of mental illness if insurance companies are telling us otherwise? Granted, blood work can't yet determine exactly how much Zoloft is a therapeutic level for me, and urine samples can't yet predict a relapse. Depressives can't yet pick up an over-the-counter depression test at Rite-Aid. But is that really what we need to have our stories be taken seriously?

I feel badly for the depressives who don't have understanding husbands, mothers, and friends who really, honestly, get it. Many can't breathe a word about their suffering to their brothers, or neighbors, or bosses.

Even more can't talk to their pastors and priests. Because a high percentage of these theologically trained and very intelligent ministers will tell a person struggling with a mood disorder to go to God alone, to read the Word, and to lay her head on Jesus. Then she can stop seeing both her psychiatrist and psychologist.

Because prayer alone is enough to heal.

In the face of such ignorance, I say this, a prayer my priest-friend Jim Martin recently taught me: "Jesus, save me from your followers." Or my secular version: "I'm sorry. My fault. I forgot you were an idiot."

Back when I was a sophomore in college, a priest preached in his homily that "the world needs God, not Valium, and that the place to go with emotional problems is the confessional, not a psychologist's office." I stood up and walked out. Every now and then I'll hear a variation of it, and I'm tempted to walk out again, but with kids that's not so easy to do.

In the psych ward—where I thought I was free of judgmental, evangelical lunatics—I was accosted by an ignorant pastor.

After the chapel service, where we read psalms and sang "Amazing Grace," he ordered me to stay put.

Pointing his holy finger at me, he said, "Honey, all you need is the Word. I was right where you are. I was down and out, too, and then I picked up the Bible and God cured me. Praise the Lord! All you have to do is believe." I was so doped up on sedatives at the time that I don't remember what I said to him, but I don't think it was nice.

The other day I came across a response to an article I wrote about depression. I have no idea who this guy is, and I'm not anxious to meet him, but this is what he said on his blog:

> It wasn't easy dealing with crazy people a hundred years ago, and it still isn't. Medication helps a lot of people and it is kind of an "Oh, shit, what do I do now" kind of solution. But here's the kicker: melancholy is a gift that this culture desperately needs. Those of melancholic temperament tend to be a little bit deeper than the average person. It is a gift and a cross that the depressive has to bear. So what do you do on the days that you just can't do anything at all? When you are so damn sick that you can't get out of bed? You ask for the strength to go on. Look at Jesus, who is on the next cross over, and cry to Him. Tell Him this really sucks and you don't want to do it. Maybe He will tell you to stay in bed. He's really cool like that and He won't push you too hard. But maybe His love will give you the strength to go on. And that's what makes a hero.

I hope his heroes stay alive longer than the ones I know. Because plenty of folks—like the Holocaust survivor Primo Levi—have perished on their knees. Peter Kramer again comes to my rescue with these words: "To see the worst things a person can see is one experience; to suffer mood disorder is another. It is depression—and not resistance to it or recovery from it—that diminishes the self."

Heck, a girl on meds can't even get a massage these days without being judged unfairly by a so-called holistic health expert.

Last summer, when I went to redeem my gift certificate for a massage that my mother-in-law gave me for Mother's Day, I walked into a holistic-healing center a bit guarded. While I consider myself to be very holistic—I engage body, mind, and soul in my recovery from depression and addiction, incorporating diet, exercise, prayer, vitamins, and so forth—I know from experience that so many of these centers espouse Tom Cruise–ish philosophies regarding medication, especially antidepressants. The large majority of these homeopathic guys believe that mental health is but one yoga class, acupuncture session, or hour of Tibetan meditation away.

I sat down at the center and filled out the health questionnaire. On page eight, I was to list all current medications. *Here we go again*, I thought to myself. When the aging hippie got to the words *Zoloft, Lithium,* and *Nortriptyline* and their hefty dosages, he frowned, obviously disappointed. Then he looked up, smiled as if had just invented Penicillin, and said, "I can decrease your need for those." As I undoubtedly expected he would say.

I processed that comment a few minutes, until, with all my clothes off, I fired away.

"Why do you say you can decrease my need for meds?"

"Massage gets blood flowing to your brain. Like exercise, it produces endorphins that can fight depression and anxiety," he explained.

I wanted to say, "Listen, dude, you don't think I know that? I only run six miles a day, soak in as much sun as the cancer experts will let me, practice mindful meditation, try every relaxation technique in the book, spend hours on cognitive-behavioral worksheets, scribble in my gratitude and mood journal, reach out to other depressives, take ten vitamins and minerals every morning plus six omega-3 softgel capsules, participate in support groups, and work on my 12-step program in order to coax every single neurotransmitter in my brain into action and rejuvenate nerve endings in specific circuits of my brain. *Do you have any idea how hard I work to stay sane?*"

I'm up on the research that affirms massage therapy and all forms of relaxation can alter brain patterns. Just as stress can kill—raising blood pressure, heart rate, muscle tension, and breathing rate—relaxation can save by producing nitric oxide, the molecule that fights cortisol and other stress hormones.

I wanted to tell him that although I adopt any and every alternative method to treat my depression, the craniosacral therapy and acupuncture sessions and magnets on my earlobes and Chinese herbs and homeopathic remedies and light lamps simply weren't enough for me. I wished to grab his peace-loving shoulders and shake him, saying, "Medication saved my life. My pills aren't like cigarettes, a habit to give up next New Year's," and to suggest that he stick to giving massages and let the neurobiologists, psychiatrists, and pharmacologists worry about the brain's limbic system, because by flapping his uneducated jaws he could very well kill one of his clients.

If I sound angry, it's for a good reason. These attitudes not only perpetuate the stigma of mental illness, they worsen the depression of millions of people around the globe. In addition to their other symptoms, depressives feel responsible and guilty for having brought on the pain themselves. And in trying to overcome it by themselves on their yoga mats, they stay stuck in the Black Hole, or resort to suicide.

Such ignorance and discrimination is why I can't assign 100 percent of the blame for the Virginia Tech tragedy on Seung-Hui Cho.

"Why the hell didn't his roommates or teachers or neighbors or family force Cho to get help?" one of my friends asked me the other day, when we were debating the topic. "It's our responsibility as a society to look after one another, and when something isn't right, to pluck that person out of the community and get him the help he needs."

"That only works," I said, "if the society is well-informed. Had I listened to my community when I was suicidal, I would be dead. Remember, they told me to get off the meds, find my center, and look to the light."

"But your community is abnormal," she countered.

"I don't think so," I replied. "Watch *Oprah* and you'll find that that philosophy is more mainstream than you think. And if it's not the anti-med, *The Secret*–esque advice to toss your happy thought into the universe and wait for it to reproduce and host family reunions (T-shirts included) inside your head, it's old-fashioned stigma against mental illnesses or cultural biases." FYI: I believe in the power of positive thinking and in the law of attraction, but I find radical interpretations such as Rhonda Byrne's *The Secret* to be dangerous, condescending, and extremely judgmental.

I reminded her that when I was a threat to myself, very suicidal and vocal about my intentions, only one person suggested I pack my bags for the hospital. She was a nurse, and not even that great a friend at the time. But because of her training she was very knowl-edgeable about mood disorders and could see some bedspread-sized red flags. Hers were the sole pair of eyes that could see the train wreck coming down the track before it happened.

The others?

Person one: "You're not depressed. You're disorganized. That's the source of your problems."

Person two: "Whatever you do, don't let this [my depression] get out. That will end your career."

Person three: "You're eating too many processed foods. Buy organic produce at Whole Foods and you'll feel better."

Person four: "You need to go back to work and get away from the kids."

Many more: "Meditate and try positive thinking."

Yes, as a society we are responsible for each other. But, man, is that scary considering what lots of folks around me believe about mental illness.

"Korean immigrants would feel shame," said Sang Lee, director of the Asian American Program at Princeton Theological Seminary, when interviewed about Cho's massacre at Virginia Tech. "There would be some reluctance and some hesitancy in admitting [a mental illness] and openly seeing a doctor."

Super.

Now we have thirty grieving families.

But American natives aren't that much more evolved in their perspective. According to J. Raymond DePaulo, Jr., MD, only one in three people with depression ever gets diagnosed and treated for depression. In one survey, 78 percent of the respondents said they would simply continue to live with depression until it passed. And of those persons who do seek help, only half of them are treated correctly, due to diagnosis errors.

Which is why, in my opinion, the first step is to educate.

Because until we count depression, bipolar disorder, and other kinds of mental illness as legitimate diseases, trying to help people like Cho won't matter. We can have the best intentions, as all of my friends and family members did, but the majority of them couldn't begin to help me because they didn't have a clue about how to recognize and treat my mood disorder.

That's why I've written this book.

As self-absorbed as I am, these pages aren't just about me. There's more to my mission than drawing attention to my bizarre cognitive patterns, and making friends and family members appreciate all the work that goes into navigating through the mountains and valleys of my brain disease.

I'm worried about what mental illness is doing to our world.

To our planet.

Whenever I start to think that I am self-serving and egomaniacal to publish my whiny thoughts in print and on the Internet when there are families in Africa with no water—when the old, reptilian part of my brain performs a PowerPoint presentation to the idle brain cells, trying to convince them that a much better use of my time would be raising money for orphaned kids in Cambodia—I need only remember the December 1998 issue of *The Economist*, which reported this: "There are 330 million people around the world suffering from depression, 90 percent of whom will not get adequate treatment. The disease afflicts more people than heart disease, far more than AIDS, and most cases are not even diagnosed." I need only recall that according to the World Health Organization, the global total of suicides attributable to depression per year is 800,000.

Moreover, if the landmark survey of over 9,000 people in 2005 published in the *Archives of General Psychiatry* was accurate in reporting that one in four adults have symptoms of at least one mental disorder each year—typically anxiety and depression—and that nearly half of all Americans suffer from a mental disorder at some point during their lifetimes with only a third of those seeking help, half of whom are incorrectly diagnosed, then a lot of people in our world are suffering.

Needlessly.

Many of them, perhaps as bright and graceful and charming and beautiful and loving as my aunt Mary Lou, who will never receive the right help.

Think about how many heroes we've lost to mood disorders, how many saints have withered with their prayer beads. Ponder for a moment how many friends and colleagues and neighbors and siblings and cousins and uncles and nephews and friends and fathers and mothers have died prematurely and cut short their lives by one bulky photo album.

Please, no more.

Not until I'm confident that if Mary Lou lived today she would be properly treated for her bipolar disorder will I stop crusading for this mission.

SANITY BREAK

On Perseverance

The heights of great men reached and kept/Were not attained by sudden flight./But they, while their companions slept/Were toiling upwards in the night.

—Winston Churchill

Fall seven times, stand up eight.

—Japanese proverb

If we are facing in the right direction, all we have to do is keep on walking.

—Buddhist saying

The greatest oak was once a little nut who held its ground.

—Anonymous

Chapter Eleven

Work It, Girlfriend!

My 12-Step Program

W hat did you do to get better?"

I hear that question a lot.

And I never know whether I should tell the truth or not . . . because I don't want to discourage anyone from pursuing recovery. Just like I tend to sugarcoat my traumatic labor story for pregnant friends.

"Does it really hurt?"

"Oh no, not really, like a bee sting maybe."

The truth? I worked at climbing out of that mass of black bile harder than anything I've worked on in my life.

And the struggle is by no means over. I continue to invest more time and energy into my mental health than any other aspect of my life—more than my career, motherhood, or marriage—because without a stable mind and body, I risk losing all of them.

How did I get better and how do I try to stay well?

Not very gracefully. Think Richard Simmons in *Swan Lake*.

Three years ago, I spent most of my time wandering aimlessly, completely lost, not knowing which voices to follow. I considered everyone—plumbers, cable guys, and US Postal Service carriers included—an expert, and I pursued all suggestions. Some flopped miserably. Like the Chinese magnets behind my earlobes I was supposed to squeeze once an hour. Hello . . . OCD? I was squeezing those puppies thirty times a minute. And I quit using my cell phone because I was afraid its magnetic charge would reverse the flow of energy, like negative yin and yang.

Other exercises worked.

They're my 12 steps: my personally designed mental-health program related to but different from the 12-step program practiced by addicts and their kin. These strategies ideally boost my neurotransmitters into action—getting those lazybones passing messages from one neuron to the next, forcing the guys to use fancy Instant Messenger or whatever it takes to grab the neurons' attention—and to inspire nerve generation and cell reproduction in the amygdala and hippocampus regions of the brain.

Step One: Find the Right Doctor

Here's one of my many book ideas: *The Psychiatric Guide to [state of your choice]: An Atlas of Shrinks.* Having a medical file with almost all the head doctors in my area, I could divulge the skinny on each one. Like which diagnosis a particular psychiatrist favors and his drug of choice: so all his patients are sent home with samples of Zyprexa, even though it is only meant to treat schizophrenia and bipolar disorder with acute mania. Oh, and persons wanting to gain fifty pounds in two months.

I'm sounding bitter, like I hate all psychiatrists, and that is so not true. The physicians who evaluated me at Johns Hopkins saved my life; I'm forever indebted to Dr. Smith for leading me to good health. But I do think that a depressive has to be *very* careful in selecting a doctor. Because she has to trust her psychiatrist with her life, and together as a team they have to maneuver through thorny patches and tackle complicated problems. As I mentioned a few pages back, Dr. Smith was my seventh doctor, and she was, as Goldilocks would say, "just right."

Here's a summary of the first six:

Doctor One: "You're a writer? Could you help me pull together a book proposal?" Truthfully, I think I offered—which is even sicker.

Doctor Two: "You're clearly ADHD, but your biggest problem is sleep deprivation. Go home, take this Ambien, even though you told me you are a recovering alcoholic and shouldn't take anything addictive, get some sleep, and check back with me in a few weeks." Later I learned that he specialized in geriatric psychiatry. No wonder he thought I had ADHD—compared to his other patients I had David's energy after eating a basket of jellybeans.

Doctor Three (Pharma King): "We're going to try a new medication every few days—until we reach fourteen in three months, at which time you'll need to go to the hospital to detox. Let's be superaggressive with these newer antipsychotics so that I can use you as a success story in my speaking gigs around the country as a psychiatrist using cutting-edge drugs. And for anxiety, pop an Ativan every half hour if you want—they're not really addictive—and a Valium or two at night. That way you won't feel a thing. You'll be so knocked out that you won't be able to cry . . . or do anything, for that matter. As a total zombie, you won't have to worry about any manic spells, which could lead to poor judgment and grave mistakes. I want you to tell me the very second you have a creative thought. Because the next thing you know, you'll wake up in a hotel room somewhere with some guy and regret what you've done. Trust me, it's better to have no personality—a perfectly even temperament—than to have highs that can ruin your life."

Doctor Four: "You have low self-esteem and you had a poor relationship with your father, so I think you have borderline personality disorder."

Doctor Five: "What do you think you are—depressed, bipolar, OCD? What would you like to take and how much? I'd love to be able to sort all this out, but the insurance folks only allow ten minutes for each patient, so you're going to have to do a bit of the diagnosing and drug selection yourself. Let's just try out some meds and see what happens. Okay?"

Doctor Six: "I know you're suicidal and all that, but let's wean you off all your meds and try some hypnotic regression using candlelight, because your condition is undoubtedly a result of childhood issues you haven't yet addressed in therapy."

Step Two: Find the Right Cocktail

I wish I could report that one doctor waved her wand once to arrive at the magical prescription that cured me. No, seven different faces waved that bloody wand twenty-three times before I found the right cocktail. But that's extreme. Most depressives have only had to try a few different medications before feeling huge relief.

Here are some treatment facts according to the Sequenced Treatment Alternatives to Relieve Depression (STAR*D) study, an unbiased investigation funded by the National Institute of Mental Health and reported in the Spring 2008 issue of the *Johns Hopkins Depression and Anxiety Bulletin* by Karen L. Swartz, one of the physicians who evaluated me in Spring 2006. I must assign a lot of power to her because I dreamed last night she was vice president of the United States and I assisted with her campaign:

- One antidepressant treatment does not fit all. You may need to try several medications to find one that works for you.
- At standard doses of the most commonly used class of antidepressants—selective serotonin reuptake inhibitors

(SSRIs)—30 percent of patients achieve remission with the first medication prescribed.

- It often takes twelve weeks to achieve an adequate response to medication, not the standard four to eight weeks that most doctors and mental-health specialists were previously using to guide decisions.
- If the first choice of medication does not provide adequate symptom relief, switching to a new drug is effective about 25 percent of the time.
- Switching from one SSRI to another is almost as effective as switching to a drug from another class.
- If the first choice of medication does not provide adequate symptom relief, adding a new drug while continuing to take the first medication is effective in about one in three people.
- People with more severe depressive symptoms and more co-existing psychiatric and general medical problems need particularly close monitoring by their doctors throughout treatment.
- Individuals who become symptom free have a better chance of remaining well than those who experience only an improvement in symptoms.
- Individuals who need to undergo several treatment steps before they become symptom free are more likely to experience a relapse. Therefore, even when the depression goes into remission, it is important to remain under the care of a physician.

Step Three: Exercise!

As a recovering addict, I am a natural buzz chaser. Any form of exercise that increases my heart rate over 140 beats per minute, or into the cardiovascular zone, does the job. And in a safe way, so I don't have to cheat on my sobriety. Working out is one mood-altering activity that doesn't deteriorate my marriage or any of my other relationships: with my kids, with myself, and with God.

Dr. James A. Blumenthal, a professor of medical psychology at Duke University, led a recent study in which he and his team discovered that among the 202 depressed people randomly assigned to various treatments, three sessions of vigorous aerobic exercise were approximately as effective at treating depression as daily doses of Zoloft, when the treatment effects were measured after four months.

A separate study showed that the depressives who improved with exercise were less likely to relapse after ten months than those treated successfully with antidepressants, and the participants who continued to exercise beyond four months were half as likely to relapse months later compared to those who did not exercise.

Even as little as twenty minutes a week of physical activity can boost mental health. In a recent Scottish study, reported in the *British Journal of Sports Medicine*, twenty thousand people were asked about their state of mind and how much physical activity they do in a week. The results showed that the more physical activity a person engaged in—including housework, gardening, walking, and sports—the lower their risk of distress and anxiety.

Exercise relieves depression in several ways. First, cardiovascular workouts stimulate brain chemicals that foster growth of nerve cells. Second, exercise increases the activity of serotonin and/or norepinephrine. Third, a raised heart rate releases endorphins and a hormone known as ANP, which reduces pain, induces euphoria, and helps control the brain's response to stress and anxiety. Other added benefits include improved sleep patterns, exposure to natural daylight (if you're exercising outside), weight loss or maintenance, and psychological aids: for example, kicking a punch bag or anything other than your boss can be a healthy way to vent pent-up anger and can help you to achieve a sense of self-mastery over your feelings . . . until the next morning, anyway.

The gym is also a kind of support group for me. These women, I'm guessing, are going after the endorphin buzz just like me because alcohol and recreational drugs don't do the trick anymore. And, like *moi*, I suspect that they also have great difficulty meditating. Every time they close their eyes, they have visions of screaming kids, Chuck E. Cheese hell, and the crisis of no thank-you gifts for teachers. Yes, the only peace available to me and my soul sisters is acquired by getting our heart rates into the fat-burning or cardio-vascular zone—running, cycling, or climbing the calories away to the Promised Land, where we will eat them up again.

Step Four: Eat Well

Last year at Christmas David cried for two hours because the state of Maine didn't say anything as he assembled his talking puzzle of the United States.

"It's not working!" he screamed, as he threw the first thirteen colonies across the family room.

"What did he have to eat today?" asked Eric.

"Christmas cookies and a candy cane," I replied. "We're sticking to the four food groups (from the movie *Elf*): candy, candy canes, candy corn, and syrup."

Lucky for me, I get to see how my brain would behave if it were a five-year-old boy. Since David and I eat basically the same diet—whatever Eric makes us—my boy's food reaction serves as a very visible and verbal alarm that we both had better return to the land of green legumes and brown grains before we throw something more dangerous than the first thirteen colonies across the family room.

Because too much sugar can be toxic to our sensitive chemistries. Last Thanksgiving holiday, I went five days without working out and four without consuming a fruit or vegetable. During the nine-hour drive home from Ohio, I could feel the neurotransmitters in my brain packing their bags for a vacation in Florida, and nerve cell connections petering out, giving the bird to certain regions of the brain . . . "See ya!"

"Wait! Wait!" I pleaded. "Don't go!" As soon as we landed in Annapolis I went grocery shopping, sticking to the outer perimeter of the store, where the broccoli and salmon are found. I also strapped on my running shoes because I wanted to say hello to my endorphins and ask them how their Thanksgiving was. I vowed to my serotonin, norepinephrine, and dopamine—to my entire limbic system—that I'd do a better job at Christmas. I'd resist the candy canes, splurge on grapefruit, and exercise five times a week.

But St. Nick came with his Yule logs and German butter cookies, and I couldn't deprive the kids of an afternoon of making gingerbread boys and Christmas-tree cookies—even if butter, sugar, and white flour were the three primary ingredients. The feel-good chemicals in my brain got ticked off again and departed.

My mouth and brain are in constant negotiation with each other because while one loves white bread, pasta, and chocolate, the other throws a hissy fit whenever they enter my bloodstream. My diet has always been an important part of my recovery from depression, but two years ago—after working with the naturopath who sold me all kinds of supplements and homeopathic remedies and reading Kathleen DesMaisons's *Potatoes Not Prozac*—I could more competently trace the path from my stomach to my limbic system. Moreover, I recognized with new clarity how directly everything that I put in my mouth affects my mood.

Here are the bad boys: nicotine, caffeine, alcohol, sugar, white flour, and processed food—you know, what you live on when you have preschoolers who won't touch tofu and spinach.

Here are the good guys: protein; complex starches (whole grains, beans, potatoes); vegetables; vitamins (B-complex, C, D, E, and a multivitamin); minerals (magnesium, calcium, and zinc); and omega-3 fatty acids.

So every morning on top of my mood stabilizer and antidepressants, I take vitamins B-complex, C, D, E, and a multivitamin, plus glucosamine, chondroitin, magnesium, calcium, and folic acid.

And I'm religious about stocking in my medicine cabinet a Noah's Ark supply of omega-3 capsules because leading physicians at Harvard Medical School confirmed the positive effects of this natural, anti-inflammatory molecule on emotional health. I treat my brain like royalty—hoping that it will be kind to me in return—so I fork over about $30 a month for the mac daddy of the omega-3s. I order online from OmegaBrite, because their capsules contain 70 percent EPA eicosapentaenoic acid (EPA). One 500mg softgel capsule—and I take six of them . . . because (my addict brain speculates) if one is good, six is better!—meets the doctor-formulated 7:1 to DHA ratio, needed to elevate and stabilize mood.

It takes me the same amount of time to swallow all my morning pills as it takes Eric to fry our breakfast eggs and set the table. But it's certainly worth the time. Because some of us really are what we eat.

Step Five: Sleep!

Sleep hygiene has nothing to do with wearing a condom and using plastic mattress liners. It's about putting your head on the same pillow, on the same bed, at the same time every night, and sleeping for the same amount of time. If that sentence just bored you to sleep, you are like me: spontaneous, erratic, unpredictable, unconventional . . .

That's why sometimes it's best to practice the advice Doc gave

Lightning McQueen in the movie *Cars*: turn left to go right. Meaning as soon as your brain says, "This is brilliant! You're on a roll! Let's stay up all night!" you need to shut down and go night-night. And vice versa, when you're in your comfy bed with a pillow over your face, and you can think of nothing worse than putting your two feet on the floor, that's exactly what you have to do, if you've slept your eight hours.

Sleep hygiene is even more complicated when you give birth to two insomniacs. Who would have thought putting your head on your pillow would be so much work? But for this manic-depressive, keeping a regular sleep schedule is truly one of the most difficult disciplines of recovery. And one of the most critical, because alterations in sleep affect circadian rhythms, our internal biological clocks, which govern fluctuations in body temperature, brain-wave activity, cell regeneration, and hormone production.

For two years I've kept a mood/sleep journal to track how my *zzzzs* affect my thoughts. This is what I've learned: less than seven hours of sleep can trigger a hypomanic cycle, which will ultimately crash into a full-blown depression, and over nine hours will generate depression. Yes, I'm that fragile.

Step Six: Light Up

My guardian angel's husband refers to his bride, Ann, as his "solar-powered wife." This sunshine-dependent woman has learned that she is a "high-intensity light" human being, a living organism that functions best when exposed to high-quality—aka Floridian or Virgin Island–ian—direct sunlight for long periods of time. When plucked from the southern beaches and planted back into her New England home, this life-form withers like so many others who suffer from seasonal affective disorder (SAD).

I'm a "high- to medium-intensity light" person myself. If I

didn't have two small mouths to feed here, I'd flock to Florida and write from there. Instead I work under a mammoth HappyLite and pretend my feet are in the sand.

Humans are like plants. Some of us require long exposures to intense sunlight while others thrive on very little. The Chinese evergreen (aglaonema), for example, requires low- to medium-light intensity, while the spider plant (*Chlorophytum comosum*) demands medium- to high-intensity sunlight.

As a depressive, I'm intrigued by the process of photosynthesis in plants—how vegetation uses sunlight to produce sugar and chemical energy—because it illustrates how powerful sunlight is to us. All of life depends on this chemical process, which uses water, light, and carbon monoxide to release oxygen. Just as a plant "puts together" (synthesis) its "light" (photo), a human sorts out the light in her environment.

After light hits our eyes, it travels through the brain to the hypothalamus—the emotional center—causing us to feel a certain way: happy . . . sad . . . or, in my case, happy, sad, happy sad, and then happy, happy, sad. Moreover, changes in the amounts of daylight a person receives alters circadian rhythms, which is why light treatment is so effective, especially for those who suffer from SAD.

And speaking of SAD, for all those naysayers who think the illness is fabricated as an excuse to head to Florida for two weeks, there was a new study just published by the National Alliance for Mental Illness (NAMI) about a possible genetic predisposition to SAD. In the study, among those persons diagnosed with SAD, seven had two mutated copies of the photopigment gene in the eye, which helps detect colors. That information may one day be used to help identify those who have a higher susceptibility for developing SAD and whether or not light treatment would be effective.

Step Seven: Reach Out!

This book is too short for me to list all the studies documenting health benefits gained by participating in support groups. The *New England Journal of Medicine* published a study in December 2001 in which 158 women with metastatic breast cancer were assigned to a supportive-expressive therapy. These women showed greater improvement in psychological symptoms and reported less pain than the women with breast cancer who were assigned to the control group with no supportive therapy. Another study in 2002, published in the *American Journal of Psychiatry*, followed a group of more than 100 persons with severe depression who joined online depression support groups. More than 95 percent of them said that their participation in the online support groups helped their symptoms.

I've been a 12-stepper for almost two decades now, but I still walk away from meetings humbled by the strength, courage, and wisdom I find in those rooms or at a coffee bar, where I'll often share my story with a fellow sister or brother who struggles with addiction and/or depression, too. And almost every day, when I log on to Beyond Blue and read the heartfelt comments of my readers, I nod my head to Martin Buber's logic, that "when two people relate to each other authentically and humanly, God is the electricity that surges between them." Can't you feel the electricity in these?

> To know that one is not alone in feeling depressed, futile and tortured is somewhat enlightening.
>
> —*Lynne*

> Very strange that two people who don't know each other can help one another in such a big way.
>
> —*Aarti*

Membership in this club to which we all unwillingly belong isn't something I would wish on *anyone*; nonetheless, reading how others have survived specific circumstances has given me hope where I'd lost sight of it and inspired me to keep on keepin' on even when my feet feel as if they're encased in buckets of cement and will pull me under the stagnant water in the bottom of the pit (the resident snakes are undoubtedly water dwellers!).

—*Margaret*

I can totally relate to the closeness that one can feel with people we "hardly" know.

—*Jacqui*

Step Eight: Get Involved

Gandhi once wrote that "the best way to find yourself is to lose yourself in the service of others." Positive psychologists like the University of Pennsylvania's Martin Seligman and Dan Baker, PhD, believe that a sense of purpose—committing oneself to a noble mission—and acts of altruism are strong antidotes to depression.

This approach certainly worked for Abraham Lincoln. Joshua Wolf Shenk, author of *Lincoln's Melancholy: How Depression Challenged a President and Fueled His Greatness,* explains Lincoln's three-prong strategy to overcoming despair:

An acknowledgement, a very clear reckoning with this pain was the first stage. Learning to live with this pain and adapting to this pain on its own terms was the second stage. Finally, the third stage was turning to a cause larger than himself and then channeling his energies and suffering to something that was bigger than he was.

This philosophy—of attaching oneself to a greater cause as a way to overcome hopelessness—is largely why I'm so committed to Beyond Blue. My blog and this book afford me an opportunity not only to creatively express myself (another happiness tool), but to give back to the world some of the gifts I have been so generously given. The personal mission statement I recently drafted as an exercise to guide my recovery said this: "I want to be an instrument of God's love and peace to everyone I meet in this world, but especially to those burdened by mental illness."

Like I said in the introduction, sharing my experience, strength, and hope is the guts of the twelfth step in traditional 12-step support programs. It's also the greatest commandment: to love God with all our hearts, minds, and souls, and to love our neighbor as ourselves. In other words, love must drive every sentence and blog post that I write, every decision and behavior throughout my day.

Lord knows I fall short of this several times a day. With two small children to feed and bathe, I can't volunteer a year of my life at an orphanage in Uganda, or dig water wells in the thirstiest parts of Africa, as a friend of mine does. But my ministry of the day—educating people about mental health—does fulfill me in a way that combats some of my blues. Because when I'm looking outward instead of inward, sometimes I forget how much I'm hurting.

Step Nine: Keep a Mood / Sleep and Gratitude Journal

Aside from maybe the Bible, my mood/sleep journal that I mentioned in Step Five is the most important book in our house. Every morning I record the number of hours I slept that night and a number to rate my mood: one being practically normal, a stabilized person who doesn't have to record every hiccup and sneeze in her day, and five being close to hospitalization—hysteria, shaking, behaving similar to the guy at the psych ward who drank the gallon of Tide.

Keeping a record of mood fluctuation allows me to discover important patterns in my temperament so that I can make the right adjustments before approaching the danger zone bordering the Black Hole. The journal does for me what a crew, or rail meat, does for a skipper trying to win the America's Cup race: reads the wind and trims the sails in order to effectively manage the movement of a boat or, in my case, a brain.

I also record in this journal all the things I'm grateful for: that I live in a free country, where I can make a career out of babbling online about my inner demons, and not in some war-torn corner of the world where women aren't allowed to talk; that I own a three-bedroom house in a gorgeous section of America, where I can spend afternoons kayaking, biking, and hiking along the elegant waterways of the Chesapeake Bay; that David hasn't noticed his talking puzzle of the United States and his walkie-talkies now live at Goodwill and that Katherine has terminated her pastime of painting kitchen cabinets with purple nail polish; that my coffee is strong, my bagel is fresh, and that the container of cream cheese wasn't filled with sunscreen or another surprise. Thank you, God, for all these things.

Even as I'm not very good at it, I know that gratitude is an effective tool to repel depression. Based on her research findings, the University of California psychologist Sonja Lyubomirsky believes that keeping a gratitude journal—taking the time to consciously count your blessings—is one of the most effective happiness boosters. According to the psychologist Robert Emmons at the University of California at Davis, gratitude exercises improve physical health, as well, including raising energy levels and relieving pain.

Dan Baker writes in *What Happy People Know*:

[Appreciation] is the first and most fundamental happiness tool. . . . Research now shows that it is physiologically impossible to be in a state of appreciation and a state of fear at the same time. Thus, appreciation is the antidote to fear.

Step Ten: Therapy and Lots of It

There are as many kinds of therapy as there are types of self-help books in my library: *interpersonal therapy*, sometimes known as crisis intervention; *psychodynamic therapy*, which focuses on a person's past in order to make sense of current problems or feelings; *supportive therapy*, which is goal-oriented and often involves strategizing about a certain conflict; *psychoanalytical therapy*, which dates back to our friend Freud and confronts self-directed anger; *group therapy*, where a small group of people with similar problems shoot the breeze under the moderation of a mental-health professional; and *cognitive-behavioral therapy*, which can be done alone or with a therapist and involves identifying and changing distorted thinking.

That's a lot of therapy.

I've benefitted most from regular sessions of psychotherapy—combining psychodynamic and supportive therapies—where I spill my guts to my counselor. Instead of looking at me like I have two heads, she jots down a few notes and then begins to help me problem-solve, to sort my challenges into a couple of different categories. Next we brainstorm about some viable solutions. By the time I hand her my credit card, my head feels lighter . . . with less junk stuffed into the corners of my limbic system. And with a few specific steps of action I aspire to do before I see her again, I often leave her office feeling empowered.

According to a study published in the *Archives of General Psychiatry*, persons with bipolar disorder who received intensive psychotherapies for up to thirty times over the span of nine months had a 64 percent recovery rate in an average time of 113 days, compared with 52 percent of those who received collaborative care, a brief psycho-educational intervention of three sessions over six weeks.

I am also a strong advocate for cognitive-behavioral therapy, the effort to reverse negative thinking and identify destructive thought patterns. Especially helpful has been *Ten Days to Self-Esteem* by David D. Burns, MD, even though it took me eleven days . . . plus a few more. He lists the following ten forms of distorted thinking, which I began to recognize in my thoughts throughout the day:

1. *All-or-nothing:* You approach everything from a black-or-white perspective.
2. *Overgeneralization:* You see a negative event as part of a constant pattern of defeat.
3. *Mental filter:* You don't take into consideration any of the positives.
4. *Discounting the positives:* You don't regard any of your accomplishments or positive qualities as legitimate. (*My college diploma was stroke of luck . . . really, it was.*)
5. *Jumping to conclusions:* You presume the worst, even without evidence. These include mind-reading (*She hates me, I just know it*) and fortune-telling (*I'm going to fail*).
6. *Magnification or minimization:* You blow things way out of proportion or you diminish the significance. (*So my husband had a few extramarital affairs and has children with all of these other women . . . no big deal . . . our kids now have half siblings!*)
7. *Emotional reasoning:* You reason from how you feel. (*I feel stupid and loopy, so I must be stupid and loopy.*)

8. *"Should" statements:* You condemn yourself and others with shoulds, shouldn'ts, musts, oughts, and have-tos. *("Stop 'shoulding' yourself!" my mom often says to me.)*

9. *Labeling:* Instead of saying to yourself, *Look, I made an error here,* you tell yourself, *My brain is bird feed,* or *I suck at everything, even insulting myself,* or *I'm as unpopular as Heidi Klum would be at an Overeaters Anonymous meeting.*

10. *Blame:* You indict yourself for something you weren't totally responsible for, or you accuse other people and assign no fault to yourself.

So after I catch myself saying something like *I'm such a loser*—"emotional reasoning" and about three other forms of distorted thinking—I will apply one of Burns's fifteen techniques of untwisting negative thinking, like "examine the evidence," to arrive at logic like this: *I may feel like a loser and yes, I haven't succeeded at absolutely everything in my life. But the percentage of people who have done so is pretty small, and, if Time magazine is accurate, those overachievers have got some pretty freaky skeletons stashed away in their closets. So, heck, maybe I'm just normal.* Or if I say, *I fail at everything,* I find something, like eating pints of Ben and Jerry's, at which I excel. Take that, bad thought!

Step Eleven: Pray and Meditate

When I was stuck in the Black Hole, I couldn't pray. I would go into my walk-in bedroom closet, shut the door, and light a candle in the dark. I stared into its flame, wanting so badly to feel at peace.

But I didn't. Instead, I trembled with anxiety, barely able to hold my rosary made of rose petals. I pleaded with God to send me a minute of consolation, to show me that He was there. I got nada.

"Be persistent," a Buddhist friend told me. "Meditation takes patience and discipline. When the distracting thoughts come, acknowledge them and then let them go. If you do this over and over again, you will begin to transcend."

It never happened. So on top of my depression and anxiety, I felt like a prayer loser. However, once I stopped trying so hard, once I quit expecting to feel a certain way or to experience a kind of mystical ecstasy, I was able to let go enough to enjoy being in the presence of God.

I pray several ways today.

Sometimes I repeat a simple mantra, *God, be with me*, as I'm walking the kids to school or pulling Katherine away from the free sausage samples at the grocery store. Sometimes those four words are enough to beat back my fear and sadness of the moment. Or I will recite a novena to St. Therese or the Prayer of St. Francis as I run my six-mile route around the Naval Academy.

Nine months ago, I started praying a rosary each morning, not because I'm an old-fashioned Catholic but because the rote prayers are easy to recite when you can't come up with anything original to say to God. There is something sacred about holding prayer beads. In fact, Christians were the last to use them, after Hindus, Buddhists, and Muslims.

I yell at God a lot, too, and I consider my loud rants prayer because getting mad and communicating my frustration means that I'm in a real, organic relationship with my Higher Power.

My prayer can be as formal as singing "Alleluia!" with a congregation of Catholics at church on Sunday, or as casual as being conscious of a divine presence as I'm folding laundry.

I don't think God cares how you pray. Because, as St. Augustine wrote: "True, whole prayer is nothing but love."

Step Twelve: Fake It 'Til You Make It

If anyone deserves an Oscar for exceptional acting, it's a depressive. My guardian angel, Ann, told me the day we met that she has spent more than half of her life pretending to be a happy person.

"People have no idea I suffer like I do. When they learn about my manic depression, they shake their heads. Because I appear to be so content and jovial."

Ah yes. *Fake it 'til you make it.* My motto.

For at least eighteen months, forty-five of my fifty-minute therapy sessions went to acting lessons: how to feign a stable and functional person until I became one.

Two days out of the psych ward the second time, I played the part of an author who was throwing a successful pub date party for the release of her book *The Imperfect Mom*, which I had compiled prebreakdown. I wanted desperately to be this person, so I visualized myself with a few good months behind me, confidently discussing the stories I had gathered before an audience of prominent editors and respected writers.

With sweaty palms and a racing heart, I sent out close to fifty electronic invitations to the classy list of contributors—like journalist Judith Newman and Baby Einstein founder Julie Aigner-Clark—and to all my publishing friends in New York, most of whom were clueless about my previous year in hell.

Five days after I sent the e-vites, my literary agent's assistant e-mailed me a list of possible caterers, wineries, bartenders, and places where I could rent coat racks and glasses.

As I read over his suggestions, I panicked.

"Oh God. Oh God. I can't do this," I said.

"What's the matter?" my sister asked. I was in her kitchen, checking my e-mails from her computer.

"This New York trip. What am I thinking? I can barely get groceries. I still cry almost every hour. I can't organize a party for all the publishing people I want to impress. What if I break down in the middle of it? They'll find out I'm crazy. My career is toast."

"Don't worry. I'll go with you," she said. "I know wines. And all we need are some cheeses, crackers, and stuff. Forget the rentals. I can put a party together. It'll be fine."

Next came the hard part: learning my lines.

"Pretend that I am an editor with *Ladies' Home Journal,*" my therapist said. "I walk up to you and say, 'Hey Therese! Good to see you. What have you been up to?' What will you say?"

"Oh. Nothing much. Just hanging out in the community room of a psych ward with Allen, an eighty-five-year-old who has slept with ninety-six women and wants to make it ninety-seven."

"Try again," she said. "You are still tutoring at the college, right?"

"Until the dean discovers a whackjob is teaching tomorrow's leaders."

"And you are writing your spirituality column, correct? There's another conversation. And your kids are always great small-talk subjects. Just stay away from the topic of depression."

On the three-hour Amtrak ride to New York, I memorized my lines, repeated them over and over again, like I was auditioning for an off-Broadway play.

I imagined the key players and rehearsed the dialogue. "Tutoring. Spirituality column. Kids. No depression."

With my sister's help, I pulled it off! I don't think anyone suspected that just five weeks earlier I was rooming with an anorexic chick, getting my vitals taken every three hours.

In fact, so successful was the New York party that I tried to repeat the act again a few weeks later, when I met a magazine editor at the Book Expo America in DC. She hugged me tightly and looked at me so sincerely as she asked me, "How are you?"

I immediately began sobbing, pig snorts and everything.

So I guess I have a bit more practicing to do before I'm Meryl Streep and become truly Oscar-worthy.

Guilt: My Confirmation Name

It's unfortunate that guilt is one of the primary tributaries feeding into the river of depression because it comes so naturally to me.

In fact, I should have chosen "Guilt" as my confirmation name—Therese Lynn Guilt Johnson (my maiden name)—because my former therapist was so impressed by my ability to feel guilty about absolutely everything that she awarded me the prestigious guilt prize. Out of all her patients in her twenty-five-plus years of counseling, I claimed the honor!

My first thoughts? *Oh no, did I take the guilt prize away from someone else? I don't really deserve the guilt prize—she gave it to me in sympathy. I should have worked harder for it. What about the starving children in Cambodia who don't get guilt prizes? I should send them mine. Why didn't I think of that sooner? How inconsiderate of me.*

I hear Jewish guilt is almost as bad as Catholic. But I think the fish-frying, saint-loving folks see the world through a guilt lens that is hard to appreciate if you haven't been yelled at by strict, unapologetic nuns.

For example, right now as I write this, I'm feeling guilty about a host of things. Like . . .

I should have picked up the house this afternoon because it's completely trashed, which could send Eric to my alma mater, the

Johns Hopkins psych unit; I haven't signed up Katherine for ballet or David for karate; I ate three Twix bars tonight; I drank four cups of coffee today; I haven't had sex with Eric in three nights so, he probably has blue balls; I haven't taken Aunt Sue out to lunch in three weeks—that was supposed to be my charity so that I don't have to feel guilty about not volunteering at the homeless shelter; I need to do more about Iraq's civil war, Afghanistan's destitution, and global poverty in general; I shouldn't have told the fifty-five-year-old nurse helping me with my MRI today that she looked *exactly* like the eighty-year-old wife of my eighty-five-year-old running partner; I haven't washed out my dog's ear like I'm supposed to; I'm contributing to global warming by using toilet paper, making coffee, taking a shower, driving to the doctor, using my HappyLite, going to the gym, and every other activity I do throughout my day; I let the kids eat too many gummies today; I should have opted for the hormone-free chicken so that Katherine doesn't get boobs before her First Communion; David is watching too much *Star Wars*—he is infatuated with the dark side; Katherine watches too many Barbie movies—I think she already has an eating disorder; I shouldn't be so candid in my writing because once the kids learn to read they will hate me; I cuss too much; I tell too many dirty jokes; I worry too much; I hate sunscreen; I feel guilty too much.

That's a modest sampling of my happy little thoughts.

My therapist suspected my acute case of self-bashing was caused by the deadly combination of three things: a strong, traditional Catholic faith; OCD and severe rumination, in particular; and the bad kind of perfectionism.

She told me to imagine myself driving a car along the highway. Whenever I get one of those guilty thoughts, my car is out of alignment . . . it's dragging right. So I pull over and assess the problem. I check to see if I need to make any adjustments. If I stole something, I should give it back. If I wronged someone, I need to make amends. Then I merge back on to the highway.

Each time my car wants to rear off the main drive, I should ask myself, *Is there something I need to do?* If not, I need to get my car back on the road.

That visualization isn't perfect, but it beats snapping my wrist with a rubber band every time I start to ruminate, which was starting to give me red marks.

Chapter Twelve

Monkey Brains

Anxiety Under Construction

The human brain is not unlike a monkey's. We have a "fear system," containing an almond-shaped clump of tissue called the amygdala. She's a real troublemaker, Amy (that's what I call my amygdala).

Amy sends an "O crap!" reaction throughout your entire body, pumping adrenaline and other not-so-great hormones into your bloodstream whenever you sense potential danger. It might be during a round of "speed networking." That's similar to speed dating, when you sit down with a stranger for fifteen seconds, or until the buzzer goes off, in which time you've divulged your entire life story and have decided whether or not the person across the table from you is your soul mate. But at speed networking, instead of swapping personal phone numbers, you exchange business cards and e-mail addresses for a networking orgy, where everyone becomes everyone else's business partner until there is only one massive monopoly in the world. Or it could happen at a conference cocktail party, hours after the speed networking, sponsored by General Motors, when you are forced to small-talk with ninety-three tables of strangers while drinking Sprite, not unlike those traumatic days in junior high when the popular girls, who were friends with your twin sister, made fun of your bad acne, and boys used you to get to your prettier, more popular sister.

A fraction of a second later, the higher, more educated, evolved, sophisticated, Harvard-professor-type region of the brain gets the signal and takes on the case, digging for the truth, sometimes accusing Amy of being an overreactive alarmist, which is almost always the case. Unfortunately we experience the fear more vividly than we do the rational response, and make decisions based on the immature brat, Amy.

The trick, then, is teaching Amy to chill out while you get the real story—a more thoughtful, considerate analysis—from the upper regions of the brain.

Amy is responsible for many of my irrational thoughts and OCD behavior.

Take the morning of my mini-triathlon.

The most challenging part of this athletic event, of course, had nothing to do with physical endurance, although I did feel like I was going to fall off my heavy mountain bike loaded with Gatorade several times as I headed into the wind.

For a person with OCD issues and a very active Amy, the real test of strength was all in the head.

Because of bacteria hang-ups I am what you would call a pool snob. The community aquatic center is not clean enough for me. In fact, sterilized conditions are so paramount for me to swim that I sought employment at the US Naval Academy just so I could use their pristine, Olympic-sized pool. Needless to say, paddling around in this "freshwater" pond the race organizers described had me a tad nervous.

When the two friends and I pulled up to the Lower Shore Family YMCA in Pocomoke City, Maryland, I nearly bailed upon spotting a brown puddle of water that looked no deeper than my bath.

"That pond out there in the front . . . is that what we're swimming in?" I asked the gentleman who gave me my race packet, feeling exactly like Clark Griswold when he arrives at a closed Walley World theme park after driving across the country in *National Lampoon's Vacation.*

"Ha! No, it's in the back."

Phew. That one would allow me to at least get horizontal without hurting my knees. But it still wasn't close to passing my contamination inspection.

Focus, I told myself. *Focus on the swim, not on how disgusting this water is.*

But when my head was fully submerged in the muddy pond a minute after the go signal, I spotted a school of small fish swimming under me.

They are only fish, I said to myself. *You are bigger than they are. Do not fear the fish. Keep swimming. Look up occasionally to see where the heck you are going, and keep swimming.*

Then more fish. And these made-for-triathlons spandex shorts I was wearing weren't tight. There was plenty of room for a fish to sneak in.

Just like Memorial Day twenty years ago.

People with OCD have great memories, unfortunately.

Our neighborhood pool held its annual Memorial Day goldfish swim, where they dumped dozens of those colorful fellows into the chlorinated water—I'm not sure how they survived—and then kids scooped them up in their plastic bags and took them home as pets.

I forget how many my twin sister and I scored that year. All I remember is that when my mom went to give us baths, my sister found a fish in her suit.

They're getting stuck in there, I know it! I panicked during my triathlon swim.

Concentrate. Focus. Swim. Do not fear the fish, for crying out loud. Ten more minutes and you're done. You'll be on your bike.

Oh my God, a big white fish! He's attacking me!

That's not a fish, you moron, that's a foot of one of the slower old guys who took off in the wave before you.

Oh God, I just got a mouthful of this filthy water! Yuck! What if I swallowed a fish?

The fish won't kill you. Not in your mouth, your stomach, or in your pants. It could not, would not. Not in a box, not with a fox. The fish can't hurt you, I say. Not in a car, or at a sleazy bar, not even if it was covered in nicotine and tar, obsessing you are! So keep on going. You're almost there.

You'd think the paranoia would end as soon as I exited the sooty pond, but not for an OCDer with an active Amy.

As I sat on my bike seat, I heard a squishing sound.

I heard the fish. I just squashed it! I knew it!

It's probably the padding in your shorts. Chill out. And even if you managed to catch one, he'll be dead by the time the ride is over.

But I can't ride 14.2 miles with a dead Nemo in my pants!

Every time I shifted gears, I thought about Nemo, wondering how he was doing. In fact, no matter how hard I tried to direct my thoughts to something else, such as the race I was participating in, I continued to freak out about the fish.

Like when I passed a chicken farm, about a half of a mile into the run.

I smell it! It's a whole family of fish, reproducing as I run! Nothing short of a fish school drying out could smell that bad!

I finally crossed the finish line singing the tune from *The Little Mermaid*: "Les poissons, les poissons, how I love les poissons!"

Which was fitting, because considering all the seaweed—but no fish!—that fell off of me in the shower afterward, you'd think I was "The Big Mermaid."

Sometimes Amy focuses on one object—like the fish—and creates a total frenzy over it. But many times she is responsible for a generalized anxiety, a tight knot in my stomach that feels, I'm guessing, like the guilt a priest or sister would experience after robbing a bank or selling condoms for Durex.

Early in my recovery I would take a sedative, or seven, on the mornings that Amy was throwing a keg party upstairs. Because a tiny seed of agitation was enough to turn and twist my thoughts into layers and layers of distortions, totally disabling me. Before long I'd be shaking nervously, unable to drive my car or load the dishwasher without holding on to something for balance.

Now I try to catch anxiety at its birth, before it has a chance to persuade my mind, body, and spirit to abandon all logic and believe the worst. I tell myself that it's just an overactive fear system—maybe Amy got a hold of some Viagra or something, that her delinquent cluster of brain tissues are sending panic messages to all my organs, that's all.

I put both index fingers into my ears and shout, "Liar, liar, pants on fire!"

Then I sit down and have coffee with the Harvard-professor part of my brain, which assists me in analyzing what is triggering such angst, and which instruments in my recovery toolbox I need to pull out in order to whack Amy over the top of the head so she doesn't start pulling me into that deep, dark abyss.

I usually come up with a few suspects in about ten minutes: an argument, even a tiny spat, that is just now reaching my limbic system and registering a message like *Alert! Someone doesn't think you are fantastic! Alert! Tomorrow you will be hated by the entire world!* Or an awkwardness in a relationship: when I have to withdraw and erect those bloody boundaries, or when I feel rejected or left out, when I didn't get asked to go to *Dora Live* with the other moms, even though the thought of dancing to a live Dora brings up breakfast.

I've been in therapy long enough to identify my two greatest fears: of my marriage failing, and of being a bad mother. When anything—an e-mail, a conversation, a news headline—or anyone touches one of those two in the slightest way, even with a feather, Amy automatically posts signs: "Toga party tonight! Everyone welcome."

For example, one afternoon Katherine at age three asked me if I had *anz-iety*. I have no idea where she picked up the word, but I'm guessing she has overheard me use this term oh, maybe a hundred times.

"*Anxiety*? Do I have *anxiety*?" I asked her.

"Yeah, do you have *an-ziety*?" she replied.

"Um. I do have a little bit of anxiety right now. How could you tell?"

"Because you're brave and ticklish. And you have poop on your head."

Her assessment was accurate. I was, at that very moment, sorting through quite a bit of crap in my brain. Two hours prior, we were visiting a friend. When my darling got restless and wanted to leave, he told me to never, ever give in to a child, that if I did, I would create a monster of a teenager—that a parent cannot raise kids with sympathy.

At the time I was too much of a people pleaser to have recognized a boundary was crossed, so I didn't tell him that I parent in my own style, and that I'm not completely responsible for the way she turns out—that she is her own person. I thought of all that later, of course, like an hour later, when I started to fume. But that's progress. A year earlier it would have taken me days to get to the fear trigger.

I suspect that Amy was parading around my head doing the bunny hop the afternoon, a year or so ago, that a good friend confided in me about her marital problems.

"You feel that way too, don't you?" she asked me.

Wanting to console her and make her feel less alone, I didn't say anything. But I should have. I should have said, "No, actually, I don't feel that way. Eric is a very supportive husband and I appreciate that about him."

Because by absorbing her problems, I made them mine. I started to second-guess my relationship, when in reality her problems didn't have anything to do with mine. She had just woken up Amy, that's all.

If it's not one of the twin fears—my marriage and my kids—Amy could be grumpy because I'm not getting enough sleep, when I'm breaking the rules of good sleep hygiene: going to bed at the same time, in the same bed, with the same man, and sleeping a consistent eight hours of sleep. Amy's also crabby whenever I shake up my routine and dare to do something different, like vacation at my twin sister's farmhouse, where one of her chickens thinks he's a dog and sleeps inside. . . . Amy gets confused, too, like the chicken. For me the slightest change—like a different time zone—can throw my neurotransmitters into a tizzy. I almost always pay a heavy toll for my binges on sweets. And, of course, when the needle on my scale starts dancing, hysteria ensues.

Many times the anxiety is a result of forgetting about my restraining order on perfectionism and his trophy wife, unrealistic expectations. I blank on all the damage the toxic pair did the last time I let them in and I again start adhering to their advice: that true happiness is found in publishing a *New York Times* best seller, which should be written in the thirty minutes of free time I have in the evening after a full day of assembling floor puzzles of the seven continents with the kids, naming each country in alphabetical order, and reading the dictionary aloud to them so that they'll perform well on the vocabulary section of the SATs in twelve years.

After I've compiled my list of suspects I come up with a game plan.

It usually involves implementing one or more of the steps from my 12-step program, which I outlined in the last chapter: like "faking it 'til I make it," pretending as if I am a normal person with a settled stomach, not about to throw up her shredded wheat with blueberries. When panicked, I try to continue writing Beyond Blue with the confidence of a woman not scared to death of a breakdown, a lady born with different chemistry.

Then I almost always try to work out extra hard—run a longer course, or swim twenty more laps—in order to give my brain an extra squirt of endorphins, which knocks Amy out with the same punch as an overdose of Ambien.

Some other strategies: I start eating things that come in their own wrappers, like apples, cucumbers, raw almonds that taste much different than the chocolate-dusted ones; I hire more sitters so that I don't have to cram so much into every minute and I can practice that good sleep hygiene I'm always talking about; I cut back on my caffeine for a day before I hike it up again, attempt to decompress by the water, spend ten minutes journaling or reading Anne Lamott, or check in with a friend or fellow depressive. A fifteen-minute phone call with Mike almost always lowers my blood pressure and can carry me halfway to sanity. He offers me free therapy.

Oh yeah, therapy. I do that, too.

I also try to remember Dr. Smith's reassuring words: that it's normal to wig out when experiencing any type of anxiety or depression in the years following a severe breakdown, but that fleeting panic and sadness usually doesn't develop into a major relapse. It just feels like it will. With more days of recovery behind me, I'll grow more resilient and better at tolerating periods of unease.

The last thing I do to tether Amy is to take out my security object. For me, it's my medal of St. Therese, but it could be anything.

I finger it every time my breath accelerates, because it's a simple way for me to do the first step in 12-step programs: admit my powerlessness over my thoughts, over Amy's noise and her low IQ, and over my insanity, so that I can give all of my monkey brain, irrational and rational, to God.

SANITY BREAK

Jesus Says to Chill Out

Scripture is chock full of "chill out," "hang tight," "I got ya covered," and "we're cool" verses. Among them:

> I tell you, do not worry about your life, what you will eat, or about your body, what you will wear. For life is more than food, and the body more than clothing. Consider the ravens: they neither sow nor reap, and they have neither storehouse nor barn, and yet God feeds them. Of how much more value are you than the birds! And can any of you by worrying add a single hour to your span of life? Consider the lilies, how they grow: they neither toil nor spin; yet I tell you, even Solomon in all his glory was not clothed like one of these. But if God so clothes the grass of the field, which is alive today and tomorrow is thrown into the oven, how much more will he clothe you—you of little faith! (Luke 12:22–25, 27–28)

Chapter Thirteen

Filling In the Gap

My SEF (Self-Esteem File)

Each summer I pick a project. The summer before last, my task was to acquire self-esteem. According to David Burns, author of *Ten Days to Self-Esteem*, that should only take a week plus three days. But two years later, I'm still not there.

From June to August of 2006, this was the routine: load up the double stroller with all floatable objects in our house—wings, inner tubes, noodles, life vests—drag them and two kids to the pool, score some beach towels from the lost and found, and plant ourselves under one of the few coveted umbrellas.

As soon as we hit the snack bar and caught up on the daily gossip from Mr. Snow Cone, I pulled out Burns's book, which is about the size of a floating raft, the word *self-esteem* taller than a fruit freeze pop. But the woman under the next umbrella was reading *ADD and ADHD for Dummies*, so I didn't feel so bad.

Then my mind would wander back to my first session with my former therapist the month before I was suctioned into the Black Hole.

"Why are you here?" she asked me.

"Because I feel like a Krispy Kreme doughnut," I replied. "I have no center." More accurately, I needed to go back into the oven because my middle still jiggled.

"The lack of self-esteem is one of the most painful symptoms of depression," writes Burns in *Ten Days*. "The central belief that causes low self-esteem is 'I'm not a worthwhile human being. I am inferior to others.'"

My problem then—and now, to some degree—is that my self-esteem is very conditional: I earn it by my accomplishments, charitable works, and popularity. Like most Americans, I subscribe to a Calvinist work ethic, which dictates that hard work is central to a person's calling and that worldly success denotes personal salvation. This perspective is groovy and peachy when life is running smoothly, because it motivates a person to strive toward her dreams.

But *oy vey* when the mind or body or spirit hiccups, and your life is running *almost* as smoothly as Greg Louganis's 1988 Olympic dive that cracked his head open, like mine was during the two years of my Great Depression.

When I couldn't contribute my skills toward some project, or volunteer my time toward a noble cause, or gain the respect of folks around me with some publishing accolade, I fell apart, into an abyss of anxiety and depression.

I'm a complete failure, I repeated to myself.

The morning I tried to convince the psych unit nurses and doctors at Johns Hopkins Hospital that I was not one of "those people" and should therefore be discharged immediately. I called my friend Mike from my hospital room in tears.

"What's happening to me?" I asked him. "I used to be successful. Remember? Our book was a bestseller. . . .

"Look at me now. I have never felt so horribly inadequate, empty, and pathetic in all my life. . . .

"When will I be able to produce something of value?

"I'm nothing if I can't write. Just a lazy and incompetent woman."

While I was on the phone, Fred, a sixty-five-year-old man who had been hospitalized for over a year, was banging his head against the wall two doors down, moaning like an injured cheetah in Namibia's grasslands.

"No . . .

"I can't take it anymore. . . .

"No . . . ," he wailed, loud enough for a nurse to run and get some sedatives to calm him down.

"Do you hear that? What the hell am I doing here?"

"Therese, listen to me," Mike said with the compassion of two Mother Teresas, a Gandhi, and the Buddha.

"You don't need to produce anything more. You've done enough.

"Put it away. None of it matters.

"Not in the end.

"You don't have to write another word," he continued. "Jesus didn't write anything. Well, maybe a few words in the sand. . . .

"You are loved as you are.

"Vickie and I are always here for you.

"We wish you peace. That's all."

I almost held my cell phone up to the headbanger's ear. Because Mike's genuine love and acceptance of me at one of my ugliest moments was worth far more than the $2,000-a-day treatment I was getting at the hospital, with no help from the insurance mafia, thank you very much.

This friend, mentor, and foster dad truly didn't care whether I became an annoying Jehovah's Witness pushing pamphlets during dinner hour, or if I put the kids in day care so that I could watch *Oprah* in my pajamas all day. It was all the same to him. He was like the Peacemaker in the beautiful Iroquois Indian tale I read in Robert Wicks's book, *Crossing the Desert*:

There was a strange and unusual figure that the Iroquois Indians called "the Peacemaker." The Peacemaker came to a village where the chief was known as "The Man-Who-Kills-and-Eats-People." Now the Man-Who-Kills-and-Eats-People, the chief, was in his wigwam. He had cut up his enemies and was cooking them in a massive pot in the center of the wigwam so that he might eat their flesh and absorb their mythical powers.

The Peacemaker climbed to the top of the wigwam and looked down through the smokehole, say the Iroquois, and as he peered down through the smokehole his face was reflected in the grease on the top of the pot. And the Man-Who-Kills-and-Eats-People looked into the pot, saw the reflection, and thought it to be his own face.

And he said: "Look at that. That's not the face of a man who kills his enemies and eats them. Look at the nobility. Look at the peace in that face. If that is my face, what am I doing carrying on this kind of a life?"

And he seized the pot, dragged it from the fire, brought it outside and poured it out on the ground. He then called the people and said: "I shall never again destroy or consume an enemy, for I have discovered my true face. I have found out who I am."

And then, says the story, the Peacemaker came down from the top of the wigwam and embraced him and called him "Hiawatha" [the name of one of the greatest Iroquois leaders].

The next day I snuck out of the psych ward, which was a cinch compared to the stunts I pulled off in high school. Eric and I strolled around the inner harbor of Baltimore patrolling the kids in case any of them got tossed into the drink like little Will.

"Do you feel like your career defines you?" I asked my other half, looking down at my hospital band, a reminder of my insanity.

"A little bit. But not nearly to the extent it does you."

Just as Eric tells me when a pair of pants adds ten pounds to my butt and my fluffy turtleneck gives the impression that I'm hiding some extra chins, he didn't hesitate to deliver his honest assessment.

"You don't have to write another word for me," he added. "I'll love you regardless."

Between him and Mike, that made two people who accepted me even if my name never appeared on anything other than a driver's license, traffic violation, and credit card bill.

If they could love this useless and unproductive person, and if God could, I thought at that moment, maybe I could try to, too.

So I picked up Burns's book and studied his model of self-esteem, which involves three levels: "conditional self-esteem," "unconditional self-esteem," and "there is no such thing as self esteem," for people like Gandhi and Buddha.

I started at the bottom, of course, with all the other Krispy Kreme doughnuts, trying to identify my strengths and weaknesses so that I could begin to accept myself based on those. To get there, my therapist assigned me the task of listing ten positive qualities about myself. I came up with two: a well-proportioned nose and thick fingernails.

At the lowest point of my depression, I was convinced that I had absolutely nothing to offer the world: that my husband deserved a wife who could load the dishwasher in under an hour and drive herself and the kids to the grocery store—one that carried half the weight, not added more—and that my kids needed a mom who could cheer them on from the sidelines of their soccer games, not one who rushed to hide behind a tree because she couldn't stop sobbing and shaking like a person with severe Parkinson's.

Everything I attempted in my professional and personal lives flopped. I would compose a sentence on the computer, read it, and delete it. After a few months of this torture, I stopped writing altogether. I canceled my column on young-adult spirituality, declined invitations to speak, and turned down opportunities to write for magazines I had been trying to break into for years.

Because I was incapable of finding anything of value in my DNA, she told me to ask four friends to make a list of my strengths.

Thankfully they identified more attributes than my nose and fingernails.

I printed out those e-mails and filed them in a manila folder I labeled as my "Self-Esteem File." Every time a person complimented me or said anything remotely positive, I added it to my SEF, which grows every time I get a kind note on a message board of Beyond Blue.

After I began to believe some of the affirmations in my SEF, such as "You could still make me laugh even when you wanted to die," and began to like myself based on those strengths, I was ready to climb to the next rung on the ladder, to "unconditional self-esteem." Explains Burns:

> You realize that self-esteem is a gift that you and all human beings receive at birth. Your worthwhileness is already there and you don't have to earn it. It suddenly dawns on you that you will always be worthwhile simply because you are a human being. It ultimately makes no difference if you are fat or thin, young or old, loved or

rejected, successful or unsuccessful. Unconditional self-esteem is freely given.

On second thought, maybe I'm not there just yet.

Here's my progress: I don't depend on professional accolades *as much* to make me feel as though I can stay in this world, and there are those moments, right after I hang up the phone with Mike or Beatriz or Ann or my mom, when I feel cool just as I am. No tales of glory needed. More often than not, I remind myself that I have a good heart, and therefore I'm doing fine.

Maybe I'll get to unconditional self-esteem *all* of the time by the summer of 2038, when I stop stealing beach towels from lost and found, gossiping with Mr. Snow Cone, and staring at the mom reading about ADHD.

As for Burns's third level—Dante's Paradise, where there is no such thing as self-esteem—that's out of reach for the foreseeable future. Not even with unlimited calls to Mike would I be so evolved as to give up the very notion of self-esteem and abandon the view that there are worthwhile persons and worthless persons. This third rung, where folks adopt a Buddhist perspective and consider self-esteem to be a useless illusion, doesn't hold many Krispy Kreme doughnuts. I mean, feeling special and needed and valued is basically everything I have ever wanted, from age zero to now. A radical step like that might feel as good as taking a humongous book on self-esteem to the pool.

Burns says it can be immensely freeing and practical. I don't know if I believe him, but this is what he says about giving up your self-esteem:

> The death of your pride and your ego can lead to new life and to a more profound vision. When you discover that you are nothing, you have nothing to lose, and you inherit

the world. Instead of worrying about whether you are sufficiently worthwhile, each day you can have goals that involve learning, personal growth, helping others, being productive, having fun, spending time with people you care about, improving the quality of your relationships, and so on. You will discover unexpected opportunities for intimacy, for productivity, and for joy in daily living.

That's a big promise. One recommendation for Burns: Could you use a 10-point typeface? I'd like to read you at the park, too, if I can do it surreptitiously.

SANITY BREAK

Love Her: My New Mantra

The following is excerpted from a journal entry in June 2005, ten weeks before I was hospitalized for the first time:

> Why is this so painful . . . finding my inner sanctuary? I'm at my sister-in-law's vacant apartment in desperate need of sleep, since I totaled a whole three hours of sleep last night courtesy of Katherine's new sleep cycle. Instead I can't stop the torrent of tears, the many conversations inside my head—what my therapist says, what my doctor says, what Eric says, what my mom says, what friends say. All the voices, the questions, the conversations, make it impossible to nod off.
>
> I feel like giving up right now. After all the medication adjustments, the therapy, the supportive friends and family, I still feel like dying. I'm so tired in this fight toward wellness, the pursuit of "normality."
>
> Medicine, I know, won't cure me. And therapy will only get me so much better. The real battle rests within me. How badly do I want it? How willing am I to yield all my instincts towards pleasing others—as a wife, mother, friend, and writer—in order to simply live?

Because when you take it all away—my husband, my kids, my friends, my career—who am I?

I sit here right now attempting to sketch her as an artist holding a pencil for the very first time.

Who am I for real? I ask over and over again, through my tears, through my breaths, through my visions of waterfalls. Take away the sense of humor, the religion, the blondish hair . . . what do you have left?

I desperately want to know so I can throw my arms around her and love her for the first time in my life.

Maybe this is my new mantra—"Love her." Because until I get there, nothing else truly matters.

Chapter Fourteen

When the World Overwhelms You and You Overwhelm the World

On Being Highly Sensitive

For the well-being of my family and for the safety of all persons involved, I adhere to a simple rule: I do not enter Toys "R" Us after 7 p.m. or when fatigued.

I am a highly sensitive person, as defined by Elaine Aron in her best seller *The Highly Sensitive Person: How to Thrive When the World Overwhelms You.* Which means that a store like Toys "R" Us and places such as Disney World, the county fair, and Chuck E. Cheese are land mines of anxiety.

For this reason I usually shop for birthday gifts in an overpriced boutique in downtown Annapolis, where I can buy puzzles made of natural bamboo shoots and feel good that I'm not adding to the landfills of plastic kids' toys.

The eve of Ethan and Delaney's birthday party, however, presented quite a predicament, as I had twenty-four hours to procure the gifts, and Toys "R" Us was the only shop open. Hence, our family made that fateful pilgrimage to what some would call Mecca as the sun set behind the Westfield Mall.

We had not been in the store for more than fifteen seconds when I was hit with the first request.

"Mommy! Goggles! We need goggles. Can we get goggles?"

"How much are the goggles?" I asked, knowing full well that

this was a trick question. If they are expensive, then the cheapskate in me says they aren't worth the dough. If they are inexpensive, which they were ($1.99), then that means I'm supporting child labor and inhumane treatment in Chinese factories.

An ethical dilemma. I hear the whimper of my daughter wanting goggles that every kid has at the pool. And I see a little Chinese boy sweating to death to make them.

"Sure, you can get the goggles."

"David wants a skateboard," Eric then said, holding a box with a helmet, kneepads, shoulder pads, and every other kind of pad short of a maxi pad.

"We can't get him everything he wants. That's how you raise spoiled, materialistic kids. He'll have to work for it."

"Therese, the kid is five years old. Let him have some fun."

"Fine. Put it in the cart."

Five minutes later the cart was full of: a Sleeping Beauty princess dress, a pink Disney princess bathing suit and matching skirt, DVDs of *Sleeping Beauty* and *Beauty and the Beast*—any hope of Katherine becoming a feminist flushed down the potty—some Lightning McQueen swimming shorts for David. Oh yeah, and the birthday gifts for which we came: a fancy lightsaber, a plastic Spider-Man on a motorcycle, and a watermelon swimsuit with matching hat.

With every item thrown into the cart I felt a tug of my heart; by making these purchases, shouts my depressed, guilt-ridden brain, I'm contributing to consumerism, globalization, landfills, pollution, child labor, materialism, and global warming.

But I kept my mouth shut. Until I was accosted by a perverted Elmo in aisle five. While rushing to the bathroom—Katherine had to go . . . *now!*—Elmo and a few of his buddies whistled at me much like a truck full of rude construction workers.

That's when I exploded.

"If we buy things from this store, our kids will not have a world to live in!" I yelled to Eric. "We are ruining our world so this bloody thing can whistle when someone walks by, which he will stop doing in three days when his batteries wear out, and then he'll be tossed in the mountain of trash with the others. All the energy—all the carbon fumes—being emitted into the atmosphere so this warped stuffed animal can catcall. And our kids are going to have to figure out what to do about it."

Eric started to laugh and then realized I was serious.

"Everything contributes to global warming, Therese. Not just goggles and Elmo. The Internet uses energy, too. (He knows I'm an online junkie.) Being prudent and doing what we can is not the same as not living."

All I could picture was that damn global warming commercial, where the guy is standing on the railroad tracks, his back to a train as it approaches. He escapes just in time, but his daughter is left to be crushed by Amtrak, or global warming. The producers of that ad must be Catholic because they mastered the guilt effect. For viewers such as *moi*, who are Catholic and depressed, with fragile wiring in the prefrontal cortex and every other corner of the brain, that commercial alone translates into at least a year of therapy sessions.

On the days that I'm fighting the grumpies, I'm like Marsha Brady picturing her mom's favorite vase getting shattered by the ball that she wasn't supposed to be playing with in the house.

When poor Marsha closes her eyes, all she hears is the words, "Mom always said, don't play ball in the house" accompanied by the image of the ball smashing the vase.

That's what it's like with the guilt of commercialism, economic globalization, landfills, pollution, child labor, global warming: the image of the train sailing down the track, David and Katherine in front of it.

Eric put his hands on my shoulders, and said, "I'm never taking you to the toy store again. You need to chill out."

Chill out.

Now there's a useless directive. Like telling this culinary-challenged wife to just go prepare artichoke bottoms and shrimp with shallot vinaigrette, or go whip up an apricot and honey-stuffed mackerel. In other words, *it's not happening.*

In fact, I couldn't read the newspaper until a year ago.

Just like feeding the ducks in Annapolis, the discipline of catching up on news requires perfect timing and some shielding—a nice wide hat or something—to protect you from all of the droppings that could potentially ruin your day.

I can't check CNN.com every half hour for the most recent headlines like Eric does. No. No. No. I'm way too anxious about the world's doom and gloom. I must wait for just the right moment: when I have a stomach full of protein and fiber, when I'm semi-rested, not too caffeinated, and when I'm not ticked off at a family member.

When all these circumstances align, which happens as often as a lunar eclipse timed with my period, I take my week's worth stack of newspapers and sit down with a cup of joe. I then inhale deeply, exhale even more deeply, and begin to read the print.

When my eyes reach headlines like "Bombings Kill 60 at University In Baghdad," or "Harsh Winter Has Afghans Struggling For Survival," or "200 Die in Darfur During Week of Intertribal Battles," or when I read that a "study by a former chief economist of the World Bank, Sir Nicholas Stern of Britain, called climate change 'the greatest and widest-ranging market failure ever seen,' with the potential to shrink the global economy by 20 percent and to cause economic and social disruption on par with the two world wars and the Great Depression," I put down my coffee mug, fold my hands, and say a prayer. And I start visualizing myself as the Michelin Woman: with padding covering my entire body to absorb the torment and affliction and to protect me from feeling too much heartbreak in a messed up world.

This sounds New Age–y, I know. It's an exercise suggested by that psychic I hired awhile back when I was totally desperate, committed to alternative therapies, and seeking any and all insight as to why I was feeling so bad. I disagree with her theory that the Pitocin used to induce my birth caused my mental breakdown. But she was very right about my needing a filter while processing news of trauma and distress.

"Imagine yourself with containers all over you," she instructed me, at which point I almost hung up. It didn't help. I still was feeling every single disappointment of every family member and friend.

I tried again and again at this visualization method. Eventually I arrived at me in the Michelin Man suit. It's far from perfect. But it does remind me to let go of the part that I can't change, like in the Serenity Prayer. Because by holding on to it, I very literally make myself sick. And while it's good and right to want to feed every Cambodian family and be a responsible steward of the earth— making "green" choices whenever possible—spending a few bucks on a skateboard for David or buying Katherine a pair of goggles shouldn't feel as though I've committed a mortal sin.

Kahlil Gibran poetically articulates where I'm going with the Michelin Man stuff, when he writes in *The Prophet*: "You shall be free indeed when your days are not without a care nor your nights without a want and a grief, but rather when these things girdle your life and yet you rise above them naked and unbound."

Elaine Aron describes a highly sensitive person as someone who is greatly affected by her environment, is very sensitive to pain, caffeine, and the overstimulation that might happen with bright lights, strong smells, and loud sirens; possesses a rich, complex inner life; is conscientious, and deeply moved by the arts; panics when she has to accomplish a lot in a short amount of time; hates loud noises and violent movies; loathes disruption in her schedule; and was often shy or sensitive as a child.

Being highly sensitive isn't necessarily a bad thing. We highly sensitive types are more intuitive and tend to be more thoughtful people because we pick up on things—like the woman crying in the back of the room—that nonsensitive persons miss or choose to ignore. According to Aron, we tend to be "visionaries, high intuitive artists, or inventors, as well as more conscientious, cautious, and wise people."

The downside of this, of course, is that we reach overarousal—not sexually, especially for those of us on Zoloft—much sooner than the average person. So, for example, when my sisters were racing from roller coaster to roller coaster and munching on cotton candy with wide smiles at Kings Island theme park, I was clinging to my mom underneath the Beast, begging her to take me home. And, while other preschool moms might fare okay at Chuck E. Cheese, I become terribly frazzled, heading to the restroom when the human-sized rats start singing. I reach a shutdown point after forty-five minutes in Toys "R" Us, especially when Elmo and his buddies whistle at me.

Along with 50 million other Americans, I have a sensitive nervous system. So, in addition to taking my meds, I turn to my seven "pacifiers," techniques and exercises that calm me down when I'm feeling like a two-year-old whose scoop of mint chocolate chip ice cream just fell off her cone, or when I don't have time to call up my mom and hear her say in her soothing mama voice, "Everything is going to be just fine."

I. Walk Away

For example, I might leave David and Katherine with Eric and walk out of Toys "R" Us before I throw Elmo and his whistling buddies across the store. Or if a conversation about global warming, consumerism, or the trash crisis in the United States is overwhelming me, I simply fake a restroom emergency. My great-aunt Gigi mastered this strategy. She recognized her triggers, and if any gossip or situation was closing in on her "activate" button, she simply put one foot in front of another and went bye-bye.

2. Close the Eyes

Ever since my mom was diagnosed with blepharospasm, I've become aware of how important shutting our eyes is to the nervous system. The only lasting treatment available for blepharospasm is surgery to permanently lift the eyelids. A person then can't shut them at all and therefore has to moisten the eyes constantly with drops. Because my mom depends on her shut-eye to regain balance and composure, she opted out of the surgery and receives regular shots of Botox instead. Her disorder is a kind of overarousal of the nervous system, so she requires plenty of alone time. When she's in a social setting, she often retreats somewhere where she can decompress.

The same goes for me.

3. Take a Break

This can be challenging if you are at work, or at home with kids as creative and energetic as mine. But highly sensitive persons need breaks to let the nervous system regenerate.

I must have suspected my sensitive disposition back in college, because three out of my four years, I opted for a tiny single room rather than going in on a bigger room with some friends. Junior year, three of my best buddies begged me to go in with them on a killer quad.

"Nope," I said to them. "Can't do it. Need my alone time, or else none of you would want to be around me. Trust me."

My senior year I went to the extreme of pasting three pieces of black construction paper on my window above the door, so that supposedly no one could tell if I was there or not, in order to get the hours of solitude that I needed. What I didn't know, and what my friends didn't tell me, was there was a rip in one of the sheets, so they could see if the light was on or off anyway.

I steal my breaks any way I can get them, which, most of the time today, happens in the bathroom or a closet.

4. Go Outside

This is a true saver for me. I need to be outside for at least an hour every day to get my sanity fix. Granted, I'm extremely lucky to be able to do so as a semi-stay-at-home mom. But I think I would somehow shove it into my schedule even if I had to commute to an office job every day.

Even if I'm not walking or running or biking or swimming, being outside calms me in a way that only the right pharmaceuticals can. With an hour of nature, I go from being a very bossy, opinionated, angry, cynical, uptight person into a bossy, opinionated, cynical, relaxed person. And that makes the difference between having friends and a husband to have dinner with and a world that tells me to go eat a frozen dinner by myself because they don't want to catch whatever grumpy bug I have.

5. Go Near Water

While watching Disney's *Pocahontas* the other day with Katherine, I realized I must be part Native American. The sheer joy of that woman paddling down the river, singing about how she is one with the water, makes me realize how universal the mood effect of water is, and especially to someone like me.

On the rainy or snowy days that I can't walk the double jogger over to Spa Creek or Back Creek, I disobey the global-warming experts and take a long shower, imagining that I am in the middle of a beautiful Hawaii rain forest. I've always needed to chill out on the side of a lake, pond, creek, or bay—even the dirty St. Joseph's River in South Bend, Indiana; or Caesar Creek State Park, the closest thing to nature near Dayton, Ohio.

My body has memory. It knows that I emerged from a womb consisting mostly of water, that all life begins and depends on the double hydrogen and oxygen combo.

6. Breathe Deeply

Breathing is the foundation of sanity because it is the way we provide our brain and every other vital organ in our body with the oxygen needed for us to survive. Breathing also eliminates toxins from our systems.

Breath work—consciously taking in deep breaths as I work at the computer, or breathing in a paper bag as I did during my panic attacks—gives me control over the fear system in the brain, and makes oxygen more accessible to every organ. Studies suggest that lack of oxygen in the brain results in negative thinking, mental sluggishness, and eventually vision and hearing decline. As far back as 1947, research has shown that when the body suffers oxygen withdrawal, normal body cells can turn into cancer cells; lack of oxygen is also a major cause of heart disease and strokes.

In the psych ward, the nurses taught us the "Four Square" Method of Breathing, which has helped me to calm down on countless occasions:

1. Breathe in slowly to a count of four.
2. Hold the breath for a count of four.
3. Exhale slowly through pursed lips to a count of four.
4. Rest for a count of four (without taking any breaths).
5. Take two normal breaths.
6. Start over again with number one.

7. Listen to Music

Back before my Prozac and Zoloft days, music was my sole therapy. I pounded away at Rachmaninoff's Prelude to C Sharp Minor as a way of processing my parents' hostile divorce. My hour or more a day at the upright piano in the family room of my childhood home became a sanctuary of sorts for me. I practiced scales, cadences, and arpeggios until they were perfect, because rhythm—that sweet pattern between sound and silence—was something that I could control with the tip of my fingers at a time when I felt so fearful, uncertain, and powerless. Emotion was translated into melody as I played the ivory and ebony keys, sometimes closing my eyes.

During the worst months of my depression, I blared the sound track of *The Phantom of the Opera*. Pretending to be the phantom with a cape and a mask, I twirled around our living room, swinging David and Katherine in my arms. I belted out every word of "The Music of the Night," which I had learned to play on the piano for my stepdad as his birthday present one year because it's one of his favorites, too: "Softly, deftly, music shall caress you, / Feel it, hear it, secretly possess you . . ." The gorgeous song—like all good music—could stroke that tender place within me that words couldn't get to.

Everything with a beat moves my spirit. Even Yanni, with his long hair blowing in the wind. But especially the classics. I can't get enough of Bach, Beethoven, and Mozart because I think much more clearly when these guys are playing in the background. Consequently almost everything I write has been composed under their influence.

Apparently I'm not alone. The Web site of the American Music Therapy Association lists fifty-seven pages of research articles chronicling the successful use of music to help treat a host of different illnesses, including depression, anxiety, substance abuse, and chronic pain.

Four Steps to Better Boundaries

In my second job out of college, I worked as a product development coordinator for a giftware company. I didn't know what I was doing. Not at all. I thought I was okay at faking it until my boss sat me down and explained that there were four stages to becoming a competent employee, and that I was at step one.

I keep thinking about those four steps because they also apply to building better personal boundaries.

1. First, you are **unconsciously incompetent**. *Say what???* Yep. You don't know how much you don't know. And your ignorance can be bliss until you get sick or suffer from stress-related symptoms like dizziness, a weird rash, or chronic fatigue. You're baffled as to why you're always run down, because you don't realize how much energy you're using in stuff that's not your problem. *I just have too much to do!* you justify. *And there is no way around it. Right?* Wrong. Time to wake up to your boundaries problem.

2. Then you become **consciously incompetent**. *Holy boundaries!* you say to yourself upon waking one day. *I have leaks of energy all over and I don't have the faintest idea how to plug them all.* Now you're getting somewhere! You can do something about your fatigue

because you've identified the problem: boundaries that look like your grandmother's window screens—with more holes than wire and totally ineffective. In 12-step language, I guess this would be the first step: admitting you have no boundaries—that your life has become unmanageable.

3. *Third, you become **unconsciously competent**.* It's a little confusing, I know. All four steps use only two words. In the third stage, you start to erect boundaries and take care of yourself but you don't realize it yet. Actually, I think this is where I am. All I know is that I'm using the word *no* a lot lately and I'm feeling extremely selfish, sometimes cruel. And yet I think I must be doing something right because I have more energy and feel a tad more relaxed. Plus my feelings of guilt have subsided a little.

4. *Finally, you are **consciously competent**.* Yah! This is the goal: to be so confident in your boundaries skills that you no longer worry about not being nice or generous. Your boundaries automatically erect in dangerous, energy-leaking situations so that you don't need to spend so much energy and time analyzing them, or whether or not you are building them the right way. The person at stage four is proof that the stuff in the Serenity Prayer is possible: accepting what you can't change, changing what you can, and knowing the difference.

Chapter Fifteen

Sorry, Wrong Number

Codependency and Boundaries

Idialed a number the other day and got the following recording: "I am not available right now, but thank you for caring enough to call. I am making some changes in my life. Please leave a message after the beep. If I do not return your call, you are one of the changes."

Not really. I didn't get that on a voice mail. My twin sister e-mailed it to me because she knows that I am constantly struggling with boundary issues.

Even in the psych ward, where you'd think you could take a brief vacation from relationship complications, I had to deal with Frank, the mentally disabled teenager who insisted that we hook up at the mall after we both were discharged.

One afternoon in occupational therapy, or recess in a psych unit, he told me I looked like Jennifer Lopez, which is as accurate as saying O. J. Simpson is Mel Gibson's identical twin. A few minutes later, as I was painting my ceramic butterfly, he handed me an ad for Gerber baby food from *Parenting* magazine.

"That's what our baby would look like," he said.

I took a deep breath.

"Frank," I responded, "I'm very flattered by your interest in me. Truly I am, because I enjoy your company very much. But while

I'm here, I really need to concentrate on not killing myself. Do you understand?"

After the nurses gave him a time-out, that boundary issue was settled.

I'm so codependent that my natural response is "I'm sorry," instead of "ouch" or "damn," when I accidentally hurt myself. One day my junior year in college, I sold my very large and cumbersome computer to a freshman for $200. Actually, that was progress! I didn't give it to her for free. I was carrying the heavy thing up the stairs of Holy Cross Hall when my hand slipped, and I fell with the solid piece of technology, the monitor and motherboard landing on three of my left toes. It hurt like a female dog.

"I'm sorry!" I automatically yelled out to the student passing me on the stairs.

She looked at me clearly confused.

"Why did you just apologize to me?" she asked.

Because . . . my father's an alcoholic? I thought.

Then I apologized for apologizing.

Currently I'm trying to retract some well-intentioned but irresponsible words I spoke a few months ago when I gave my bleeding heart a voice: i.e., placed an order of problems to be delivered rush, for no extra coast, to my house.

A lady I met in church has severe arthritis and is in a lot of pain. She also suffers from depression. One day I took her out to lunch, gave her a big hug and said, "If you ever need to talk, come on over."

So she did. Almost every day. I began having lunch with her a few times a week, which didn't exactly fit into my schedule: packing thirty working hours into ten hours of child care; therapy, doctors' appointments, my twelve-step program; volunteering at the kids' schools, organizing Katherine's play dates, supervising David's homework and activities; and attempting to say hello to Eric every once in a while.

As usual, my body scolded me—I got sick—and advised that I erect some boundaries ASAP before I catch something more serious than a cold.

Did I drive over to the woman's house and tell her, "I'm sorry, but what I really meant was that you are more than welcome to come knock on my door once or twice a month and stay for about a half hour"?

No.

"Kids, for the next three days or however long it takes me to learn good boundaries, we have a new policy when someone comes to the door," I said, as I pulled down the blinds to the window in the foyer. "We wait until Mommy peeks out of the kitchen window to see if it's safe to answer it. Understood?"

"So that we don't open the door for any bad people?" David asked.

"Well, kind of like that," I answered.

I've classified this dilemma with similar predicaments under a category that I have termed "The Good Samaritan Complex"—a quest to become the generous, kind-hearted gentleman in Luke's parable, not the evil, self-absorbed Levite or priest in the story.

My version of the parable goes like this:

> Lady Codependency was on her way to work one day when a beggar asked her for change.
>
> "Come join me for breakfast," she said, wanting desperately to please God. She treated the beggar to a huge Au Bon Pain feast.
>
> For the next month, he stalked Lady Codependency on her way to work. Prince Not-So-Codependent, Lady Codependency's husband, finally logged onto MapQuest to find an alternative route for his codependent bride.

Lady Codependent struggled to find a way to be both compassionate and street savvy. Following the suggestion of a friend, she bought a packet of McDonald's certificates to hand out to beggars, hoping to ensure that none of her money went to drugs.

But the first recipient attacked her verbally. "I don't want your f———coupon! What's the matter with you, lady?" he screamed.

A few months later, Lady Codependency was exiting her favorite coffee shop with a medium cappuccino in her hand, feeling especially guilty for indulging in this pleasure while others suffered.

"Ma'am, Ma'am," a middle-aged woman called out to Lady Codependency. "This is an emergency, Ma'am. I need $2.50. I just had a miscarriage. I need some women's stuff."

As codependent as she was, Lady Codependency was not a moron. She was 99.9 percent sure the woman was high, really high, on some drugs that Lady Codependency sort of wished she could get her hands on. And she didn't appreciate the woman using the excuse of a miscarriage to get cash if she, in fact, hadn't had one. The chances of that were great. This smelled like a scam stronger than Lady Codependency's cappuccino smelled like heaven. But if there was a .01 percent chance that this woman were telling the truth, Lady Codependency would have spent $2.50 on her coffee but not on a person in need. She thought about Luke's Gospel, and, dang it, she wasn't going to be that Levite. So she handed the woman the money.

The woman immediately ran off to her friends, giggling and laughing.

One week later, some boys selling magazine subscriptions rang the doorbell at Lady Codependency's residence.

"We're trying to improve our chances of having a life

like you do: a house, kids, and so on," they said to her with droopy eyes like Lady Codependency's lab/chow mutts when they were mere puppies. She felt her bleeding heart about to burst all over whatever they were going to sell her. She longed to invite them in, give them her checkbook, take them to Au Bon Pain, and order some clothes for them from llbean.com.

"Could you just please buy a magazine from us?" the guys begged her.

"Of course," Lady Codependency replied, and ordered a subscription to *Parenting* magazine for the bargain price of $50, a mere $38 more than a regular-priced subscription.

The next day, the same woman who asked Lady Codependency for $2.50 because of a miscarriage approached her again.

"Ma'am! I just ran out of gas. Ma'am, this is an emergency! Can you spare me some money?" she asked Lady Codependency.

"You hit me up yesterday," said Lady Codependency, quite disillusioned from her attempts at compassion, and wondering if maybe the Good Samaritan had some codependency issues himself and needed to do some boundary-building exercises and go to therapy.

Pulling the blinds, at least temporarily, on my needy friend was, no doubt, the pansy's way of erecting boundaries. But you have to start somewhere, and I got a rather late start in learning how to "use my words," as I say to David and Katherine twenty times a day. Unlike Eric, who vocalizes a resentment before it's had time to fester and start a family, I hate confrontation so much that I'll befriend the resentment—dress it up, take it out on the town, hang out with it for years—anything to avoid conflict.

On some level, I fear that any conversation of substance will end the same way as the one I had with my dad two decades ago—when I conjured up the courage to tell him how hurt I was that he missed my high-school graduation. (He was golfing.)

He responded defensively. "Of all the things I've done for you," he said, "you have to concentrate on that?"

I tried one more time, a year later, to tell him I wanted a better relationship with him. Newly sober, I was struggling with all the drinking in our family.

"Dad," I asked, "would it be possible for you not to drink around me?"

He followed through—by excluding me from family trips, where my sisters and he bar-hopped all night.

Those are ugly snapshots of my dad. And before I give you the impression he was an insensitive, horrible, and abusive man that single-handedly caused my depression, let me say this: my dad was brilliant, and incredibly driven, witty, charming, determined, creative, insightful, sensitive, and loveable.

His disease of alcoholism, however, wasn't.

And although I have made progress at distinguishing the disease from the person, thanks to attending 12-step support groups and reading codependency literature, some deep scars remain from the rejection I felt in my early years.

Pepper those scars with memories of my mother's severe depression after my dad left—her devastation through big chunks of my childhood, when we switched roles and I mothered her—and you've got yourself a certified codependent and a person destined for a real Messiah fixation.

I don't mean to "blame the parents," the oldest psychology trick in the book and one I fully endorsed until I became a mom. Because my mom is certainly one of my mental-health heroes. And I'm just now beginning to appreciate many of my dad's extraordinary talents—saving money and networking, for example—that I didn't fully respect while he was still alive. His death at the ripe age of fifty-six from a bronchial pneumonia, the year after I graduated from college, put all of his qualities into proper perspective. Resentment faded as I realized how much I loved and admired him. However, I can't help but agree with the theory psychologist Harville Hendrix posits in *Getting the Love You Want*: that in our relationships, and especially in our love relationships, we will unconsciously re-create the past in order to try to heal childhood wounds.

According to Hendrix, the trick is learning to distinguish between the messages of the old brain and those of the new brain.

The old brain includes the brain stem, responsible for physical actions, and the limbic system, which determines our automatic and unconscious reactions, usually generating vivid emotions. The new brain is the cerebral cortex, home to most of our cognitive functions and a whole lot smarter than the old, reptilian brain. Writes Hendrix: "The new brain is inherently logical and tries to find a cause for every effect and an effect for every cause. To a degree, it can moderate some of the instinctual reactions of your old brain."

That is, my old brain says to me, upon meeting my church-lady friend, "You absolutely need to solve her problems. By taking her to lunch, you will feel whole and needed, just like when you told your mom it would be okay, everything would be fine, and that Dad would come back one day. Absorbing the church lady's pain is the path to a divine dugout much like your mama's womb, when you were without a single request or frustration, where you experienced the original wholeness you've been after ever since you exited the crowded place with your twin sister. So go pick her up right now!"

My new brain says: "Therese, I'm not so sure that's a good idea. Let's do the math. You've got five deadlines today to complete in two hours of baby-sitting. If you try to grind out your articles while you watch the kids and supervise homework, you will probably yell profanities. Right? That always happens. And when the short people start repeating your profanities, you will feel like a horrible mom, at which point you'll pick up the phone to call Mike or your mom for a much-needed affirmation, to hear you are an okay mom, and while you're after that warm fuzzy the midgets will discover a new hobby: gluing last year's art projects to the white walls. Why not skip lunch with the church lady and get your work done so that you can be June Cleaver without the pearls or tuna casserole with the kids when they're home."

Recognizing the idiotic memos from my old brain is basically the same thing as identifying the voice of my Attachment Hunger, a concept Howard M. Halpern writes about in his insightful book *How to Break Your Addiction to a Person*. He argues that those of us who didn't get our attachment needs met as infants and/or toddlers suffer from Attachment Hunger in our adult years. That drives us to addictions to other people, or in my case, to everything I encounter.

"To the degree that your parents gave you gratification in the attachment phase and then, after about the first year and a half, supported your independence, you will have less of a hangover of Attachment Hunger in your adult life," Halpern writes. "To the degree they failed to be helpful either in the attachment phase or the launching phase, you may have intense residue of needs from the Attachment Hunger level that can compel you to seek and cling to relationships in an addictive way."

By recognizing my Attachment Hunger and telling that babe to pipe down, I prevent the hurt in my past from ruining my present and future, from trapping me in dysfunctional, codependent behavior.

Whenever I start to obsess about an unhealthy relationship in my life, when the Infant in me tries to persuade me that I absolutely need a certain someone in my life—that we need to exchange e-mails ten times a day plus regular phone calls—because our communication is the difference between drinking Folgers instant coffee in the morning and a Starbucks double espresso, I tell the baby to hand over his rattle, because I'm sick of the noise.

Then I will sketch a bottle of vodka in my journal, and I will write the person's name on that bottle: to remind myself that the craving for the dysfunctional relationship, that the obsessions about the person, is just a different kind of addiction, a type of self-destruction that will deplete my reserves of self-esteem and leave me feeling even more empty inside.

There have been so many times in the two decades that I have been sober that I've had to say to the Infant inside of me, "Look, dude, Huggies stopped making diapers at size six (50 pounds). It's time you learn how to *grow up!*" And there have been even more times that I've had to be rescued by fellow recovering addicts and wise friends who can identify the whine of the colicky baby inside me, to help me see with accuracy the flawed messages of that brat, especially when I'm most vulnerable.

With every month of recovery I'm better able to gauge when I'm in Infant Time and when I'm wearing pull-ups, but I'm certainly not yet free from the pain of wishing for something that isn't there. The late theologian Henri Nouwen must have been camping out inside my head when he composed these lines in his book *The Inner Voice of Love*:

> Intellectually I knew that no human friendship could fulfill the deepest longing of my heart. I knew that only God could give me what I desired. I knew that I had been set on a road where nobody could walk with me but Jesus. But all this knowledge didn't help me in my pain.

As I begin to love and respect myself more—and as I depend more and more on God to satisfy my inner void—I've begun erecting boundaries in many of my relationships. I'm choosier with whom I befriend because I can now recognize when I'm being treated unfairly or without respect. I feel less need to stick around just to keep the water calm.

Nor can I afford to share myself with everyone who comes along. That's too dangerous and wearing—with pieces of your soul left out to dry on too many doormats. I need to surround myself with people who are working just as hard as I am at staying well and positive, resisting the plethora of opportunities to turn to the Dark Side and talk trash and gloom.

I feel much like Anne Morrow Lindbergh, who wrote in *Gift from the Sea*, "I shall ask into my shell only those friends with whom I can be completely honest. What a rest that will be! The most exhausting thing in life, I have discovered, is being insincere."

However, even as I'm beginning to know what I need and want, the processes of saying no and of erecting the proper boundaries still feel as uncomfortable and awkward as wearing a too-big wetsuit backwards. I know because I have done that. The thing is bulky and restricting; it draws in water and makes you sink.

However, if I keep on practicing my boundary-building skills, one day I will find that, like a wetsuit that fits perfectly, I am staying buoyant with little effort of my own. The boundaries will assist me in conserving energy for the persons and things in my life that I love, all the while protecting me from the nasty jellyfish and the chilling temperatures of the bay . . . or a bad relationship.

One day I will intuitively know how to say no and not feel guilty. *All right, that's a stretch.*

One day, my guilt in erecting a boundary will last one day, maybe even a few hours, not the year or more it does now.

I'm taking baby steps toward becoming a more sincere person. I'm inching toward the person who will not have to temporarily pull down the blinds on a needy friend, who won't feel guilty for not giving two bucks to a scam artist, who uses her words as easily as her kids have learned to, who says "ouch," not "I'm sorry," upon dropping a heavy computer on her toe, and who can heal her Attachment Hunger with enough positive, supportive relationships, plus the guy upstairs. And even in its awkwardness, that feels good.

Use Your Words

When you use your words, you learn a lot about people and their priorities. You invite responses that are downright ugly and difficult to hear.

That's why I hate using them.

But silence isn't the solution. Not if you want to keep your cortisol levels low. The trick is using your words with absolutely no expectation of what kind of response you'll get. *Yeah, right.* You say them for the sake of expressing them, not for anything you hope to hear. If that's at all possible.

I distinctively remember the first time after my big breakdown that I made a conscious effort to voice my frustration.

I had just graduated from the hospital outpatient program with lessons in effective communication fresh on my mind. The psychiatric counselors taught us that stress and anger stoke each other, and that left alone for too long, they'd get restless inside your brain, triggering excess adrenaline and cortisol that do bad things to every organ in your body.

Cross-eyed Katherine was sitting on my lap inside an ophthalmologist's office. We had already seen a doctor who told me that my two-year-old would absolutely need surgery. But I wanted a second opinion.

"When did you first notice her crossing her eyes?" asked Dr. A.

"This summer," I responded.

"Is it snowing outside?" he asked.

I looked out the window. "Yeah, it is."

"What have you been doing for the last six months?"

You really want to know, asshole? I thought to myself. *Munching on stale Salisbury steak in the community room of Laurel Regional Hospital's psych unit with some other folks in hospital robes because I have trouble dealing with mean people like you.*

"Actually, we've already seen one other ophthalmologist," I explained calmly. "But I wanted to get a second opinion, and it took three months to get an appointment with you."

He continued Katherine's evaluation, but I couldn't let it go. I was fuming inside.

"You know, your comment about the snow," I said. "I don't appreciate your suggesting that I am a slacker mom. Because I'm not."

"I'm sorry if I offended you," he replied. "I was just getting you back for your joke about the diaper." Katherine had pooped as soon as he walked in and I asked him if his joint was a full-service operation . . . if he changed diapers.

"Well, there are some things I'm sensitive about," I explained, "and being a good mom is one of them."

The hospital counselors would have been proud. I think I decreased my adrenaline and cortisol by a few notches. And later on, by the way, I discovered that Dr. A is not only an excellent ophthalmologist but also a kind person, as long as you don't mention diapers. He even laughed when I told him that this story made it into my book.

Chapter Sixteen

Risking Intimacy

Sex, Marriage, and Depression

Adepressive has more than a few things working against her in the bedroom. Up until a few months ago, I would have vowed the sexual side effects of SSRIs to be the most debilitating of handicaps. According to Andrew Goldstein, MD, and Marianne Brandon, PhD, cofounders of the Sexual Wellness Center in Annapolis and co-authors of *Reclaiming Desire: 4 Keys to Finding Your Lost Libido*, approximately 40 to 70 percent of women on these medications report one or more of the following: low libido, inefficient or unsustainable arousal, vaginal and/or clitoral numbness, and difficulty achieving orgasms.

In the past, whenever Dr. Smith asked me how I was tolerating the sexual side effects of Zoloft, I'd be flip with my response. I was ecstatic to be coming out of my severe depression and euphoric to think that I might even become a functioning part of society— able to work, drive, and pick up my kids from school without a wad of Kleenex in my jean pockets.

"Who cares about the sexual side effects?" I would tell her in all seriousness. "I don't want to die anymore! I wake up and can breathe on my own without using a paper bag! It's taken me a year and a half and twenty-three different medication combinations to get here. I'm not going to chance it all for a measly orgasm."

She would mention some alternatives: switching to Wellbutrin, which has a lower rate of sexual side effects, experimenting with a "drug holiday" or changing the time of day I take my Zoloft, or adding Viagra to my mix of medications.

I was so petrified, however, of getting sucked back into the Black Hole that I was content just to give Eric his sex twice a week and not to expect mutual satisfaction.

Having been on SSRIs since I turned nineteen has been a handy excuse for not having to explore my sexual self and take the risks that doing so requires. When Dr. Smith mentioned seeing a sex therapist, I laughed out loud. Picturing Rozalin Focker, the sex therapist in the 2004 comedy *Meet the Fockers*, I envisioned Eric and I blowing into each other's ears, massaging each other's feet, and holding hands as we sat in a circle of other copulation morons at a sex camp in Vermont.

I blamed my below-zero libido on the stress and sleep deprivation of being a mom to two extremely active kids while trying to maintain a career. After all, flat sex drives can be expected in this period in a woman's life: "David hit me!" "My milk spilled!" "Can you wipe me?"

I need only make some sarcastic crack about my lagging libido at the neighborhood park to learn that intercourse is certainly not the preferred form of recreation for the young mom crowd, and that my orgasm is hardly the only one that ran away from home.

Just the other day, I eavesdropped on this conversation between four attractive moms in their late thirties and early forties:

"I'm telling you, I hate it!" one said.

"I can tolerate it if I'm not tired," chimed in number two.

"I force myself to do it for him," added another.

"Not me. I've got to want something bad in exchange for that," said the last.

Were these ladies talking about: 1) eating raw carrots without ranch dressing, 2) scrubbing down public toilets, 3) chaperoning a camping trip of thirty Girl Scouts, 4) going on a one-week cruise with their in-laws, or 5) having sex with their husbands?

Answer: 5.

A recent survey by Harris International showed that 52 percent of Americans sixteen and older are not fully satisfied with their sex lives. The majority of those with lazy libidos are women. In fact, some health professionals believe that low libido and diminished sexual desire have become a new epidemic in our society. Orgasmic disorders—where women either have never experienced an orgasm, called primary anorgasmia, or seem to have lost their ability to experience one, called secondary anorgasmia—affect approximately 25 percent of the female population in the United States.

One out of every four women freezes up in the bedroom like I do.

Are they all popping Zoloft?

I doubt it.

After some considerable soul-searching and a few teary sessions of psychotherapy, I've come to understand that my most significant sexual and relationship problem—the reason why I have difficulty letting myself be touched and aroused, to be sensual and playful—is a hiccup far deeper than a stymied libido. It's rooted in my fear of intimacy.

Good sex, for most evolved human beings, requires intimacy.

And nothing scares me more than intimacy.

Because to be intimate with a partner is to risk rejection. To become absolutely vulnerable. Clothes off. Naked. Nothing between two persons.

I'm only now confronting and processing the profound rejection I felt from the single most important man in my life until Eric: my dad. I didn't realize how the repeated message of rejection—whenever I'd beg him to attend a piano recital and was told to stop whining, or when I'd inquire about one of those mysterious, monthlong business trips and was blown off—seeped into my subconscious and began to program a love life that was destined to fail.

Howard M. Halpern writes in *Cutting Loose: An Adult's Guide to Coming to Terms with Your Parents*: "The parent-child relationship is a primary source of who we are, and the mutual emotional attachments are derived from countless interactions, conscious and hidden memories, and profound feelings that go back to our days of oneness with them."

Our childhood experiences, says Halpern, are recorded in our brain cells. These feelings, thoughts, and responses—including fear, joy, insecurity, inadequacy, love—are deeply channeled and have worn pathways of behavior that are hard to reverse. So in the years a person survived a dysfunctional mess, her thoughts carved a cognitive path in order for her to preserve her sanity and feel safe. But the longer she lets the older, reptilian part of her brain do the thinking for her—loaded with videotapes of hurtful childhood experiences—the harder it is for her to change the direction of her responses and behavior as an adult.

My dad possessed countless admirable traits. But among them were not "nurturing father" and "devoted husband." And those were the only ones that mattered to me as a ten-year-old. So the lesson continually recorded into my little-girl brain was that men were unreliable at best, callous bastards at worst.

By the time my dad officially left my mom, when I was in fifth grade, I was a bona fide man hater.

In hindsight, it makes sense that for the first third of my life, I would aspire to be a nun, a missionary in India, who could live her life independent of all men, except for the pope, who has a pretty good reputation. I now realize why I came home crying from a ballet once because, as I explained to my mom, I wanted to dance like that, too, but I didn't want some pervert holding me up in the air. I understand now why I ended up at an all-women's college, why I pursued unavailable men in high school and college, and why I'd sabotage any meaningful relationship lasting more than a few months in the days before I met Eric.

With a few positive dating experiences as a teenager, I might have come to view men as potential partners, complex but ethical human beings who struggle with their consciences just as much as women do with theirs. Perhaps I would have acknowledged how unfair it was to label every person belonging to the male species as a criminal: charged guilty until proven innocent.

But the traumatic event of St. Patrick's Day, 1988, only confirmed my prior suspicions that men don't have hearts or souls.

They have penises.

That was the morning I awoke on the slimy floor of a college ghetto house and later saw that my underwear was stained with blood. After some investigation my girlfriend swore to me I wasn't raped. That was the official report from her brother's friend.

But, as I explained to my therapist the other day in tears, even if nothing happened that night, my memory still holds in its impressionable brain cells the horror I felt at that moment. And the three weeks following the incident: nervously waiting for my period to come, hoping to God that no one penetrated me, and that if someone did at least the episode wouldn't result in a pregnancy. Even if the college guys left me alone, that doesn't diminish the shame, the self-hatred, the self-disgust I absorbed into my fragile adolescent psyche that day.

Now I've read at least half of the self-help books on the market today. I've spent ten years in therapy. And my day job involves promoting mental health. But I never once shared this high-school story to anyone—not even to Eric—until very recently, because

I have always assigned 100 percent of the blame to me. I was the idiot who drank too much and passed out in a green miniskirt at a frat house. What did I think would happen?

Not until I read the chapter "The Hidden Impact of Sexual Trauma" in Goldstein and Brandon's *Reclaiming Desire* was I able to classify what happened to me as a teenager as sexual trauma, which the authors define as "any unwanted sexual advance, whether verbal or behavioral, that leaves a person feeling victimized and exposed."

As many as one in five girls or women suffers from some form of sexual trauma. And the numbers would be much higher if every woman traumatized actually recognized and classified her experience as such. "Incidents that don't meet the legal criteria for sexual abuse still can have a traumatic impact," write Goldstein and Brandon. Like me, many women dismiss traumatic episodes as no big deal—high-school stupidity or a really bad date. Many feel entirely responsible for what happened. So they bury it and stuff it and then bury it some more until their intimacy shield is so thick—allowing no one in—that some detective work is inevitable. Only then are they forced to contemplate why they prefer to watch an episode of *Sex and the City* over the real deal, why their bodies can't function the way science books say they should, and why their relationships don't feel safe.

Obviously sexual trauma can't explain all of the flat libidos in American bedrooms. There are a myriad of different possibilities that could go wrong in one or both persons: hormonal imbalances, chronic fatigue, poor body image, depression or other mood disorders, and, of course, stress. Satisfying sex is more complicated and entails more work than dropping by Victoria's Secret.

How, exactly, does one reclaim her sexual desire?

Goldstein and Brandon say this:

Ultimately, reclaiming your sexual desire is about finding the balance that is necessary for your life energy—your essence—to flow freely. Sometimes a blockage stems from a physical problem, like a hormonal imbalance in the body or a neurochemical imbalance in the brain. It might evolve from an emotional problem, such as depression or low self-esteem. A lack of intellectual stimulation or spiritual fulfillment can dampen sex drive too.

Regardless of where a blockage originates, it can feed into other imbalances over time. . . . Attention to all the elements that drive your life energy—physical, emotional, intellectual, and spiritual—is necessary for sexual desire to return.

If you're as imbalanced and broken as I am, you may have interpreted those last two sentences like this: *I'll never ever orgasm.* Read on, though:

Rest assured, you don't need to achieve absolute balance among the physical, emotional, intellectual, and spiritual components of your sexuality and your self in order to reclaim your desire. You can want sex again without resolving all the underlying issues that may be affecting your libido. For most women, the simple act of consciously and fastidiously attending to the need for balance is enough to bring about change.

I still need a few more months of solid recovery before I'm comfortable tweaking my meds—switching from Zoloft to Wellbutrin—in order to reduce sexual side effects. And, although I've read the studies on how Viagra is safe and effective for women, a part of me doesn't want to join Bob Dole's club quite yet. I may very well enroll in sex school, benefiting from a few sessions with a sex therapist at the Sexual Wellness Center here in Annapolis.

But most important, I'm trying to teach myself, with a combination of psychotherapy and cognitive behavioral therapy, that intimacy is possible, especially within a loving marriage like mine, and that I need not fear it anymore. The worst is over. Done. I can move on.

True intimacy makes for great sex.

Even if you're on Zoloft.

SANITY BREAK

On Marrying a Head Case

Eric has come a very long way in understanding what it means to be married to a person with a mental illness since my first severe panic attack in the spring of 2005.

On that afternoon some years ago, David was pretending to play hockey, wearing a pair of my black high heels as skates, using a plastic bat as his stick, and the cap of a peanut jar for the puck. One-year-old Katherine was, of course, naked, and chasing him around.

I suddenly felt dizzy and grabbed a chair to sit down. My heart started pounding and I began to shake. I couldn't breathe, as if I were trekking up Mt. Hood with a serious buzz. I searched for oxygen as David rummaged around for his hockey puck.

I'm going to die! I thought to myself. *I'm having a heart attack!*

"Inhale . . . one, two, three, four. Exhale . . . one, two, three, four," I repeated until I caught my breath about fifteen minutes later. I still felt like I was in a fishbowl, separated from the outer world by a layer of glass. *I am alive, right?* I pinched my hand to make sure.

I phoned Eric at work and asked him to come home.

By the time he arrived I had resumed a normal breathing pace, but I was still sweating and shaking.

"What's the matter?" Eric asked me. "You look okay."

"But I'm not. I'm really not," I replied.

I explained the panic attack, how I felt like I was suffocating or having a heart attack, that I wasn't in control, not in the least bit, and that I was afraid to be with our kids when I felt this way.

It was hard for me to describe what I was feeling when I didn't really understand what was happening myself. So Eric and I learned together, as most couples do when one person is diagnosed with an illness.

There are those times—when the black dog of depression mistakes my brain for a tree and the dizzy spells of anxiety have me too scared to leave home—that I've had to remind my groom that he married a head case, a woman with extra-fragile wiring and a shrinking hippocampus. But more often it is he who taps me on the shoulder to say, "That fifth cup of coffee might not be great idea, and why don't you leave the preschool fund-raising to a mom with more neurotransmitters than you."

Because of Eric's commitment to me and to our family, and because we both invest an incredible amount of energy into our communication, I'd like to think we'll find ourselves outside of the 90 percent of marriages where one person is bipolar that ends in divorce, and that we'll be able to defy the statistic that claims people with bipolar disorder have three times the rate of divorce and broken relationships as the general community.

This, I know: I am alive today in large part because of my mate.

Chapter Seventeen

The Least Harmful Addiction

(Because I Have So Many)

There is a reason why smokers who want to quit should never diet as they come down off the nicotine addiction. For one, they will lose friends and family. But also, because there is only so much self-control available in one head. We humans have a limited amount of willpower. It's like coal.

I'm not making this up to rationalize all my addictions, although I am pleased to have some science with which to gag the self-critic who postulates that there is no reason why I shouldn't be able to master home-work boundaries, pitch the frozen bags of Kit Kats, ban all baked goods, lay off the booze, outlaw cigarettes, cut out all diet soda, work out five times a week, decrease my meal portions, limit my kids' TV time, and walk the dogs at lunch.

When I do finally go out and try to relax with some friends, I'm supposed to savor my sparkling water with a—oh yeah, baby, bring it on—slice of lime!!!!!

Like everything in life, willpower is a learned skill, a mental muscle that people need to exercise, says Roy Baumeister, a psychology professor at Florida State University who led a study on the relationship between self-control and glucose levels. Says Baumeister in a 2008 Sydney Symposium on Social Psychology:

Self-control . . . depends on a limited resource (akin to the folk notion of willpower and character strength). The analogy of self-control resource to a muscle is confirmed with several sets of findings. . . . One important aspect of self-regulatory resources is the level of glucose [aka Hershey bars] in the bloodstream, which produces the fuel for brain activity and which appears to be closely tied to acts of self-control.

What all this means for me: each morning presents an opportunity to live addiction free. And by breakfast—first addiction: caffeine—I decline that invitation, hanging on to at least three major addictions from my list. Because, come on, you heard the professor, we all have crutches and, I'd add, anyone without them is as dull as David's scissors: they don't cut anything—and their only purpose is to trigger temper tantrums from preschoolers.

If something feels good, chances are great that I'm addicted to it, because, as Craig Nakken explains in *The Addictive Personality*, "addiction is a process of buying into false and empty promises," and I've never been capable of recognizing scams. So I try to manage my addictions with a policy that I call "the least harmful addiction."

Like a drill sergeant I line up my vices in order of most threatening to least threatening, and that order is always changing. The key players are as follows: depression, caffeine, sugar, workaholism, alcoholism, toxic relationships—bet you didn't know that they raise your blood pressure, weaken your immune system, and increase your chances of heart disease and diabetes—and nicotine.

For example, today was mostly a success: I inhaled a rather large Hershey chocolate bar, drank four cups of coffee, and checked my e-mail and Beyond Blue messages constantly. I stayed free of the more dangerous killers: booze, cigarettes, dysfunctional relationships, and depression.

I guess I just try to be pragmatic in my recovery, which is like a four-story apartment: The ground floor is survival—literally keeping myself alive; the second level, staying out of the psych ward; the third deck is status quo, meaning not getting worse; and the final tier is moving toward health.

Translation: When I was severely suicidal two years ago, getting drunk wouldn't have been the *worst* thing I could have done. Killing myself would have been. Many days I contemplated getting hammered, if only to escape the pain for an hour. I knew, on some level, that getting plastered wasn't a permanent solution and would make me feel even worse. But still, it would have been better than swallowing the twenty bottles of pills stashed in the garage that I was seriously considering.

At very difficult times in my sobriety, I have gone on smoking binges. That's not healthy behavior, right? But it beat the bottle. For me a box of Marlboro Lights was much less dangerous than a shot of vodka, and it carried me through the acute craving for alcohol and back to level three (status quo).

There have been a few days in my life, maybe five, that have been addiction free, hours that I have lived like Jesus or the Buddha or Mother Teresa. During these seasons, I was sunbathing on level four—blasting to a healthy new me. And then I accidentally walked into some hornet's nest and I grabbed for the coffee or the computer or the Kit Kat. Oh well. Not a huge deal in the big picture.

But lest my readers think I'm contracted by the Dark Side to encourage addictive behavior and rationalize all weaknesses, here are a dozen addiction zappers and depression busters I use in deficient moments. They are a personalized toolbox that I created with the help of my therapist—strategies to direct me toward mental health, and an emergency lifeline in case I get lost along the way. I consult these techniques when I panic or get pulled into addictive behaviors; moreover, they are my armor in my ongoing war against negative thoughts.

I. Get Some Buddies

It works for Girl Scouts and for addicts of all kinds. I remember having to wake up my buddy to go pee in the middle of the night at Girl Scout camp. That was right before she rolled off her cot, out of the tent and down the hill, almost into the creek. Had the roller's buddy not been such a deep sleeper the Girl Scout wouldn't have woken up in the woods.

The same method works for addicts—to help each other not roll out of the tent and into the stream, and to keep each other safe during midnight bathroom runs. My buddies are the six numbers programmed into my cell phone, the voices that remind me sometimes as many as five times a day, "It will get better."

2. Read Away the Craving

Books can be buddies, too! And when you are afraid of imposing like I am so often, they serve as wonderful reminders to stay on course. When I'm in a weak spot, and my addiction has the power—dangling me upside down like Rosie O'Donnell in her inversion therapy swing—I place a book next to my addiction object: the Big Book goes next to the liquor cabinet; some 12-step pamphlet gets clipped to the freezer, where I store the frozen Kit Kats; William Styron's *Darkness Visible* or Kay Redfield Jamison's *An Unquiet Mind* rest on my bedside table; and I'll get out Melody Beattie before e-mailing an apology to someone who just screwed

me over. And there are my spiritual staples: books by Henri Nouwen, Thomas Merton, Anne Lamott, and Kathleen Norris.

3. Be Accountable to Someone

In the professional world, what is the strongest motivator for peak performance? The annual review. Especially if you're a stage-four people
pleaser like I am. You want nothing more than to impress the guy
or gal who signs your checks. Twelve-step groups use this method—
called accountability—to keep people sober and on the recovery
wagon. Everyone has a sponsor, a mentor to teach them the program
and to guide them toward physical, mental, and spiritual health.

In my early days of sobriety, I didn't drink because I was scared
to tell my sponsor that I had relapsed. She was intimidating, which
is why I chose her. Today several people serve as my "sponsor," keeping me accountable for my actions: Mike, my therapist, Dr. Smith,
Beatriz, Fr. Joe, Deacon Moore, Eric, and my mom. Having these
folks around to divulge my misdeeds to is like confession: it keeps
the list of sins from getting too long.

4. Predict Your Weak Spots

When I quit smoking, it was helpful to identify the danger zones—
those times I most enjoyed firing up: in the morning with my java,
in the afternoon with my java, in the car, and in the evening with
my java and a Twix bar.

I jotted these times down in my "dysfunctional journal" with
suggestions of activities to replace the smokes: In the morning I
began eating eggs and grapefruit, which don't blend well with cigs.
I bought a tape to listen to in the car. An afternoon walk replaced

the 3:00 smoke break. And I tried to read at night, which didn't happen. Eating chocolate is more soothing after tucking in a three-year-old girl who tells you after bedtime prayers that she knows how to kiss like Princess Leia and she likes it a lot.

Especially difficult were the times Eric and I went out socially, when my cigarette was a substitute for drinking. I think I devoured sweets on those evenings—which isn't optimal, but, again, chocolate is a less-threatening addiction to my health than nicotine, so it wasn't the worst thing to do.

5. Distract Yourself

All addicts would benefit from a long list of "distractions," any activity than can take her mind off of a cig, a glass of merlot, or a suicidal plot during severe depression. Some good ones: crossword puzzles, novels, sudoku, e-mails, reading Beyond Blue; walking the dog, card games, movies, *American Idol*—as long as you don't make fun of the contestants (bad for your depression, as it attracts bad karma); sports, cleaning out a drawer, a file, or the garage . . . or just stuffing it with more stuff; crafts like sewing, scrapbooking, framing pictures; gardening—even pulling weeds, which you can visualize as the colleague you hate working with; exercise, sitting outdoors, and music.

6. Sweat

Working out is technically an addiction for me according to some lame article I read, and I guess I do have to be careful with it since I have a history of an eating disorder. But there is no addiction zapper or depression buster as effective for me than exercise. An aerobic workout not only provides an antidepressant effect, but you look pretty stupid lighting up after a run or pounding a few beers before the gym. I don't know if it's the endorphins or what, but I just think much better and feel better with sweat dripping down my face.

7. Start a Project

Here's a valuable tip I learned in the psych ward: the fastest way to get out of your head is to bury it in a new project—compiling a family album, knitting a blanket, coaching Little League, heading a civic association, planning an Earth Day festival, auditioning for the local theater, taking a course at the community college.

"Try something new!" the nurses advised us as we chewed our rubber turkey. "Get out of your comfort zone."

I knew that Eric would love it if I became more domesticated— actually notice the dying plants and do something like watering them or pulling off the dead leaves. So, partly to please him, I went to the arts and crafts store and bought twenty different kinds of candles to place around the house, five picture boxes for all the loose photos I have bagged underneath the piano, and two dozen frames. Two years later, all of it is still there, bagged and stored in the garage.

However, I also signed up for a tennis class, because I'm thinking ahead and when the kids go off to college, Eric and I will need another pastime in addition to reading about our kids on Facebook. I met a friend with whom I trained for a triathlon—which distracts and burns calories simultaneously—and I enrolled in a writing class, which gave me enough confidence to launch Beyond Blue. If I weren't training for a triathlon and writing Beyond Blue, I might be smoking and doing a few other less-than-healthy activities as I try to organize our pictures.

8. Keep a Record

One definition of suffering is doing the same thing over and over again, each time expecting a different result. It's so easy to see this pattern in others: "Katherine, for God's sake, Barbie doesn't fit down in the drain—it's not a water slide!" or "Samantha, I hate to break it to you, but quitting your job isn't going to solve your drinking problem." But I can be so blind to my own attempts at disguising self-destructive behavior in a web of lies and rationalizations. That's why, when I'm in enough pain, I write everything down—so I can read for myself exactly how I felt after I had lunch with the person who likes to beat me up as a hobby, or after eight weeks of a Marlboro binge, or after two weeks on a Hershey-Starbucks diet. Maybe it's the journalist in me, but the case for breaking a certain addiction, or stopping a behavior contributing to depression, is much stronger once you can read the evidence provided from the past.

9. Be the Expert

The quickest way you learn material is by being forced to teach it. That lesson is fresh on my mind this morning after an hour of tutoring a student on a paper about the history of the Supreme Court. Sometimes that's how I feel about Beyond Blue—in cranking out spiritual reflections and mental-health secrets, I have to pretend to know something about sanity even if I feel like one crazy and warped chick. I adamantly believe that you have to fake it 'til you make it. And I always feel less depressed after I have helped someone who is struggling with sadness. It's the twelfth step of the 12-step program and a cornerstone of recovery. Give and you shall receive. The best thing I can do for my brain is to find a person in greater pain than myself and to offer her my hand.

If she takes it, I'm inspired to stand strong, so I can pull her out of her funk. And in that process, I am often pulled out of mine.

10. Grab Your Security Item

Everyone needs a blankie. Okay, not everyone. Mentally ill addicts like myself need a blankie, a security object to hold when they get scared or turned around. Mine used to be my sobriety chip. Today it's a medal of St. Therese that I wear as a necklace or carry in my purse or in my pocket. I'm a bit of a scrupulous, superstitious Catholic, but my medal gives me such consolation, as does St. Therese herself, so it's staying on my necklace or in my pocket or purse. It reminds me that the most important things are sometimes invisible to the eye: like faith, hope, and love. When I doubt all goodness in the world, and accuse God of a bad creation job, I simply close my eyes and squeeze the medal.

11. Get on Your Knees

This would be the addiction virgin's first point, not the eleventh, and it would be followed by instructions on how to pray the rosary or say the Stations of the Cross. But I think that the true addict and depressive need only utter a variation of these two simple prayers: "Help!" and "Take the bloody thing from me, now!"

12. Do Nothing

If you do nada, that means you're not getting worse, and that is perfectly acceptable most days. After all, tomorrow is another day.

Epilogue

I, Too, Have a Dream

In celebration of Martin Luther King, Jr.:

I have a dream that one day I won't hold my breath every time I tell a person that I suffer from bipolar disorder, that I won't feel shameful in confessing my mental illness.

I have a dream that people won't feel the need to applaud me for my courage on writing and speaking publicly about my disease, because the diagnosis of depression and bipolar disorder would be understood no differently than that of diabetes, arthritis, or dementia.

I have a dream that the research into genetics of mood disorders will continue to pinpoint specific genes that may predispose individuals and families to depression and bipolar disorder (like the gene G72/G30, located on chromosome 13q), just as specific genes associated with schizophrenia and obsessive-compulsive disorder have been located and identified.

I have a dream that brain-imaging technology will continue to advance in discovering what, exactly, is going on inside the brain, that a neurological perspective coupled with a biochemical approach to mental illness will develop targeted treatments—new medication and better response to particular medications—so that we can cut out that painful trial-and-error process.

I have a dream depressives won't have to risk their jobs in divulging their condition, that employers will respond more empathetically to the country's 7.8 million working depressives, that the general public will be more educated on mental illness so that it doesn't cost this country more than $44 billion each year like it does now.

I have a dream that families, friends, and coworkers will show kindness to depressives, not reproach them for not being stronger, for not having enough willpower and discipline and incentive to get well, for not snapping out of it, for not being grateful enough, for not seeing the cup half full, for not controlling their emotions.

I have a dream that tabloids like *In Touch Weekly* won't lump allegations of Britney Spears's taking antidepressants into the same category as her twenty-four-hour marriage, all-night clubbing, and pantyless photos—that our world might be more sophisticated and informed than that.

I have a dream that people will no longer use the following terms to describe persons with mental illness: *fruity, loony, wacky, nutty, cuckoo, loopy, crazy, wacko, gonzo, nutso, batty, bonkers, ditzy, bananas,* and *crazy,* unless the depressive, and *only* the self-proclaimed depressive, opts to describe herself and not anyone else with those words in order to add a touch of levity to discussions about mental illness and to emphasize the role of humor in healing.

I have a dream that spiritual leaders might preach compassion to persons with mental illness, not indict them for not praying hard enough, or in the right way, or often enough, and that judgmental New Age thinkers who blame all illness on blocked energy in chakras one through seven might be enlightened to understand that fish oil, mindfulness meditation, and acupuncture can't cure everything.

I have a dream that health insurance companies will stop serving Satan and read a medical report every now and then, where they would learn that depression is a legitimate, organic brain disease, and that those who suffer from it aren't a bunch of weak, pathetic people who can't cope with life's hard knocks.

I dream that one day depression won't destroy so many marriages and families, that 90 percent of marriages where one person is bipolar *won't* end in divorce and people with bipolar disorder *won't* have three times the rate of divorce and broken relationships as the general public, that better and faster treatment will work in favor of every form of intimacy.

I have a dream that suicide won't take more lives than traffic accidents, lung disease, or AIDS, that together we can do better to reduce the 30,000 suicides that happen annually in the United States, and that communities will lovingly embrace those friends and families of persons who ran out of hope, instead of simply ignoring the tragedy or attaching fault where none should be.

I have a dream that one day depression, bipolar disorder, and all kinds of mental illness will lose their stigma, that I won't have to whisper the word *Zoloft* to the pharmacist at Rite Aid, that people will be able to have loud conversations in coffee shops about how they treat their depression in addition to the excellent dialogue on Beyond Blue.

Mostly, I dream about a day when I can wake up and think about coffee first thing in the morning, rather than my mood—is it a serene one, a panicked one, or somewhere in between?—and fretting about whether or not I'm heading toward the black hole of despair. I dream that I'll never ever have to go back to that harrowing and lonely place of two years ago. That no one else should have to either. But if they do, or if I do, that they not give up hope. Because eventually their tomorrow will be better than their today. And they will be able to dream again, too.

Recommended Reading

Aron, Elaine N. *The Highly Sensitive Person: How to Thrive When the World Overwhelms You*. New York: Broadway, 1997.

Baker, Dan, and Cameron Stauth. *What Happy People Know: How the New Science of Happiness Can Change Your Life for the Better*. New York: St. Martin's, 2004.

Bradshaw, John. *Home Coming: Reclaiming and Championing Your Inner Child*. New York: Bantam, 1990.

Burns, David D. *Feeling Good: The New Mood Therapy*. New York: Avon, 1999.

———. *Ten Days to Self-Esteem*. New York: HarperCollins, 1993.

DePaulo, J. Raymond, Jr., and Leslie Alan Horvitz. *Understanding Depression: What We Know and What You Can Do About It*. New York: John Wiley & Sons, 2002.

DesMaisons, Kathleen. *Potatoes Not Prozac: Simple Solutions for Sugar Sensitivity*. New York: Simon & Schuster, 2008.

Dowling, Colette. *You Mean I Don't Have to Feel This Way? New Help for Depression, Anxiety, and Addiction*. New York: Bantam, 1993.

Goldstein, Andrew, and Marianne Brandon. *Reclaiming Desire: 4 Keys to Finding Your Lost Libido*. New York: St. Martin's, 2004.

Halpern, Howard M. *Cutting Loose: An Adult's Guide to Coming to Terms with Your Parents*. New York: Fireside, 1996.

———. *How to Break Your Addiction to a Person*. New York: Bantam, 2003.

Hendrix, Harville. *Getting the Love You Want: A Guide for Couples.* New York: Holt, 2001.

Jamison, Kay Redfield. *Exuberance: The Passion for Life.* New York: Vintage, 2005.

———. *An Unquiet Mind: A Memoir of Moods and Madness.* New York: Vintage, 1997.

Kramer, Peter D. *Against Depression.* New York: Penguin, 2006.

———. *Listening to Prozac: The Landmark Book About Antidepressants and the Remaking of the Self.* New York: Penguin, 1997.

Nakken, Craig. *The Addictive Personality: Understanding the Addictive Process and Compulsive Behavior.* Center City, Minnesota: Hazelden, 1996.

Nonacs, Ruta. *A Deeper Shade of Blue: A Woman's Guide to Recognizing and Treating Depression in Her Childbearing Years.* New York: Simon & Schuster, 2006.

O'Neill, Cherry Boone. *Starving for Attention.* New York: Continuum, 1982.

Pauley, Jane. *Skywriting: A Life Out of the Blue.* New York: Ballantine, 2005.

Rapoport, Judith L. *The Boy Who Couldn't Stop Washing: The Experience and Treatment of Obsessive-Compulsive Disorder.* New York: Signet, 1989.

Seligman, Martin E. P. *Authentic Happiness: Using the New Positive Psychology to Realize Your Potential for Lasting Fulfillment.* New York: Free Press, 2002.

Shields, Brooke. *Down Came the Rain: My Journey Through Postpartum Depression.* New York: Hyperion, 2005.

Solomon, Andrew. *The Noonday Demon: An Atlas of Depression.* New York: Scribner, 2001.

Styron, William. *Darkness Visible: A Memoir of Madness.* New York: Vintage, 1992.

Thompson, Tracy. *The Beast: A Journey Through Depression.* New York: Plume, 1996.

———. *The Ghost in the House: Motherhood, Raising Children, and Struggling with Depression.* New York: HarperCollins, 2006.

Acknowledgments

First and foremost, I want to thank Michelle Rapkin, my editor and my very good friend. If she had not been born, this book, as it reads now, would not be in print. Because the feedback I received from the publishing world was to "try to sound more normal." When I told this to Michelle, she gasped. "Oh God, no! No, Therese! Whatever you do, *do not go normal on me!*" And then she said (she was unemployed at the time), "I'm going to get a job as an editor so that I can buy this book and keep your voice as it is." She followed through on her promise, and four weeks later, Claudia (my agent) called me with an offer.

More important, though, than buying this book and shepherding it through production, Michelle authored 90 percent of the notes that fill my self-esteem file. She e-mailed me an affirmation *every day for a year* during the worst of my depression. Her phone number was one of the six I had programmed into my cell phone as voices of logic and love when I wanted so desperately to die.

The other five deserve mention as well.

Mike, my writing mentor and foster dad, gets credit for everything I write well because I learned the craft from him. He helped me to find my voice with a straightforward memo he e-mailed me ten years ago called "Leach's Rules for Revisions." Two years ago, when I stumbled upon my real, authentic self, he exclaimed: "Yes! That's it! Right there!" Of course, finding your voice requires finding yourself, or being able to accept yourself in a way I thought impossible until I met him. Mike's unconditional love toward me has inspired me not only to write better but to love better.

My mother—who prayed to St. Therese, the Sacred Heart, and to Mary for a year for me—is another one of my six numbers, as is my best friend, Beatriz, who routinely reminded me about the strength I had back in college to stay sober on a campus full of drunks. My aunt Gigi, who had been through her own nervous breakdown in her thirties, shared with me all of her recovery tools. I know that Aunt Gigi is praying for me from heaven because the morning of her funeral was the first time since the horrible anxiety descended that I didn't have to use a paper bag to breathe. After Aunt Gigi died, my twin sister, Trish, replaced her as one of the six programmed into my cell phone. Sharing a womb with someone makes you pretty tight, and Trish, well, she was incredibly loving to me my year of hell, as were my other two sisters. Finally, there is my guardian angel, Ann, a stranger I met on Amtrak who became a guiding light in my darkest hours and a true luminary who held my hand when I was afraid to open my eyes.

I must thank my agent, Claudia Cross, who has become a dear friend in the four years we've worked together. I mean, how can you not love a woman who not only agrees to read your stuff *and* represent you, but also ships pints of ice cream to your home when you've had a nervous breakdown? All that plus a postcard from Paris to say that she had said a prayer for me while kneeling in front of a statue of St. Therese at an old church there: that I'd find peace, and that our book would help others.

Mammoth hugs to Priscilla Warner, my new best friend, my director of publicity and promotions, and my copy editor, who spent almost as much time on this book as me. Priscilla was incredibly generous at every stage, offering all of her editorial and marketing expertise as a *New York Times* best-selling author. And if that's not enough, she's also the artist and jeweler who designed my St. Therese necklace, which has become my new blankie (security object).

And speaking of publicity, a heartfelt thank-you to Superwoman herself, Caren Browning of the Morris-King Company and her army—Sherry Kasten and Rebecca Freed—who managed to book me on a gazillion radio shows and some national TV shows, getting the word about Beyond Blue on the airwaves whenever possible.

Thanks to Fr. Joe Girzone, the priest who first inspired my vocation to write after I finished reading his best seller, *Joshua*, back in college. Miraculously he reappeared in my life just as I began to surface again, and he was there to encourage me and support me in my new ministry.

Thanks to one of my other dear priest-friends, Fr. Dave Schlaver, who introduced me to the world of publishing back at Saint Mary's College, and who fortunately (for my career) refused to publish my horrid poetry that I shoved in his face while I was there. Speaking of Saint Mary's, thanks to my three good professor-friends there for all they have taught me: Keith Egan, Phyllis Kaminski, and Joe Incandela. And also thanks to my dear high-school religion teachers, Stan Trohah and Carleen Suttman.

A tremendous thanks to my editor at Beliefnet, Holly Lebowitz Rossi, who is my silent partner on the job and should be given much of the credit behind Beyond Blue's success. Let me borrow Eric's phrase and say that Holly was and is my "urine when I can't pee." She's that important. She is largely responsible for my raw, frank writing. "Real, Therese, be real and write from where you are . . . not from where you want to be," she tells me. When I have the guts to follow her advice, good things happen (to good people).

All of the folks at Beliefnet, my mothership, deserve a hearty thank you. Especially Debbie Caldwell. She took a huge chance on Beyond Blue back when she assigned me a test blog for two weeks in October 2006. When it officially launched two months later, she was behind me 100 percent, as she truly believed in its mission and my voice.

Thanks to Beliefnet's Matthew Melucci for helping me to stretch myself into the video-blogging and social-networking world. Not only did Matt take an hour of his busy day to explain (over the phone) where, exactly, I could find the videocam on my laptop, he was always there for a pep talk when I needed it, cheering me on and reminding me to stay as real as possible.

Thanks to all my other Beliefnet cheerleaders. Without these supporters, I might be self-publishing (not that there's anything wrong with that): Michael Kress, Elizabeth Sams, Steve Waldman, Amy Cunningham, Rebecca Phillips, Valerie Reiss, Patton Dodd, Jenn Sturiale, Wendy Schuman, Laura Sheahan, Nicole Symmonds, Ansley Roan, and Lilit Marcus. Thanks, too, to John Kennedy and Gus Lloyd of Sirius Radio, who made a regular spot for me on their show, and became friends after a year or so of my jabbering on air about all kinds of topics, as I hid myself from the kids in the garage on Tuesday mornings with a cup of coffee.

Thanks to John Thomas and Lisa Biedenbach, for all the professional coaching along the way (such as, "Enough of the compilations! What could you possibly 'like' next? 'I Like Compiling Essays So I Don't Have to Write Anything Original and Face Rejection'? Enough already. Get out there!").

Thanks to Joani Gammill, the only person in my life enlightened enough (as a nurse) to know that I needed to be hospitalized, and to my late aunt Mary Lou (my godmother) whose suicide taught me about the dire consequences of not taking mental illness seriously enough, and whose loving memory has commissioned me to forever work toward educating people on mood disorders and how to treat them.

Thanks to my first therapist, Nancy, who started me on this journey and had the guts to ask me the hard questions. And immense hugs to my current therapist, Nancy, who has made the process to some of those answers less frightening. Thank you for empowering me with solutions and some amazingly creative visuals on how I can master my thoughts, and for your sincere compassion and support at a few critical crossroads.

Thanks to my psychiatrist, Milena Hruby Smith, positively the best head doctor in Maryland, Delaware, and Virginia (I've seen most of them), for guiding me toward health.

Thanks to Maggie Heim, babysitter extraordinaire, who watched David and Katherine lots of hours and was extremely creative in keeping their attention as I plugged away at this book upstairs.

Thanks to my very dear Beyond Blue readers, who inspire me with their courage and insight, and who are the reason I'm so excited to log on to the Internet every day.

Thanks to all the folks at Center Street who have devoted their time, skills, and energy to produce this book.

And, thank you, Eric. For everything. Especially for loving me.

Index

ABOUT THE AUTHOR

Therese J. Borchard is the author of the hit daily blog Beyond Blue on Beliefnet.com, which is featured regularly on the Huffington Post and was voted by PsychCentral.com as one of the top ten depression blogs; she also moderates the popular group Beyond Blue on Beliefnet's social-networking Web site. Therese is the editor of *The Imperfect Mom: Candid Confessions of Mothers Living in the Real World*, which has been featured in *Real Simple, Parenting, More, Working Mother, Psychology Today, Fit Pregnancy*, the *Chicago Tribune*, and on Salon.com; and of *I Love Being a Mom: Treasured Stories, Memories, and Milestones*, a Target selection that has been featured in *Redbook, Parenting, BabyTalk*, the *Chicago Tribune*, and the *Detroit Free Press*. With Michael Leach, she is coeditor of *I Like Being Married* and the national bestseller *I Like Being Catholic*.

Therese has published articles in the *Washington Post, Ladies' Home Journal, Parenting, American Baby, Guideposts, Publishers Weekly*, the *Baltimore Sun*, and *America*, as well as on the Huffington Post, Yahoo!, and PsychCentral.com. Her nationally syndicated column, "Our Turn," is distributed biweekly by Catholic News Service. She appears monthly on Sirius Satellite Radio, is featured regularly on radio programs throughout the country, and has been a repeated guest on national television programs, such as *Fox and Friends* (Fox News Channel) and *Politically Incorrect with Bill Maher* (ABC).

But scratch all of that. Because it's not very important. Who is the woman responsible for penning the bizarre content in between these covers? A female whackjob merely trying her best to stay sane by swimming lots of laps, meditating by the water, and sleeping eight hours a night with her husband and, on most nights, her two children in a very cluttered and chaotic house located in Annapolis, Maryland. You wouldn't want to visit. Trust me.

For more information, visit www.thereseborchard.com.